More Praise for *KickStart to College*

"At a time when the college application process is getting more and more demanding and complicated, it is wonderful to have a book like *KickStart to College* to help guide you along the way. It provides so much useful information, so many great ideas, and very clear explanations about how to handle the entire college process from an early beginning. This book covers everything!"

—Mark Anestis, College Hill Coaching, Fairfield, Connecticut, and author of *5 Steps to a 5 on the Advanced Placement Examinations: Biology*

"As the parent of a ninth grader, *KickStart to College* opened my eyes. I am now armed with the information necessary to approach the college experience earlier rather than when it is too late to try and do the right thing."

—Katy Dobbs, editorial director, Weekly Reader Custom Publishing

"Marian Borden's book is the most complete guide to college admissions. Whether you are a student-athlete or just a student, this is the book for you. This book is the best step-by-step manual I have read. From the admissions process to obtaining an athletic or academic scholarship to applying for need-based financial aid, she leaves no questions unanswered."

—Ralph Polson, associate head soccer coach, College of Charleston

KickStart
to College

KickStart to College

Marian Edelman Borden

ALPHA

A Pearson Education Company

International Standard Book Number: 0-02-864370-4
Library of Congress Catalog Card Number: 2002106331

04   03   02   8   7   6   5   4   3   2   1

Interpretation of the printing code: The rightmost number of the first series of numbers is the year of the book's printing; the rightmost number of the second series of numbers is the number of the book's printing. For example, a printing code of 02-1 shows that the first printing occurred in 2002.

Printed in the United States of America

For marketing and publicity, please call: 317-581-3722

The publisher offers discounts on this book when ordered in quantity for bulk purchases and special sales.

For sales within the United States, please contact: Corporate and Government Sales, 1-800-382-3419 or corpsales@pearsontechgroup.com

Outside the United States, please contact: International Sales, 317-581-3793 or international@pearsontechgroup.com

For my mother-in-law, my friend
Edith S. Borden

and

For my son, my favorite writer,
Samuel E. Borden—

with all my love and appreciation.

Contents

Getting (Kick) Started

There are many good college admission books—and if you look at the end of this one, you'll find an annotated listing of the best.

So the question is this: Why do I think you needed something different?

Bottom line (and you'll find these throughout the chapters): None of the books on the market begin at the right time. I don't want to worry you, but frankly, if you hit your junior year of high school and are just beginning to consider college, you're about three years too late. That's not to say that you can't make up the time, or that you've already made too many mistakes to overcome. But the truth is, students need to start thinking about college while they are still in middle school.

Obsess over college admissions when you're only 13? Absolutely not. But there is a lot of territory between obsessing and ignoring, and middle school is the ideal time to be realistic about college as you ...

- ✏ Plan your high school academic career.
- ✏ Choose your extracurricular activities.
- ✏ Decide on summer experiences.
- ✏ Prepare for standardized testing.
- ✏ Most of all, if you haven't already done so, it is the time to take school seriously—very seriously.

Does this mean that your life should be just about preparing for college? No. Life's too short—have some fun.

But can you have some fun and still get into the college of your choice? You bet. And be sure to notice that I said the college of your choice. This book is all about choices—your choices. I don't want you to get to your senior year and say "If only ..."

- ✏ **If only I had picked the right courses ...** Read this book and you'll find out why the classes you choose for eighth grade will affect the courses you can take your senior year in high school.

- **If only I had found an extracurricular activity I liked** ... This book will tell you how to find the clubs you like, why extracurricular activity is important to your own development, and, secondarily, how to make it sound interesting to colleges.
- **If only I had done something besides getting a great tan during the summer** ... This guide will tell you how to enjoy the vacation months, grow as an individual, make some money, and impress colleges.
- **If only I had gotten better scores on my standardized tests** ... You'll find out from the experts what standardized test scores mean, score points in the admissions game, and how to improve your own results.

Once we get through talking about making the most of your high school days—and, again, that's so they are fun and productive (notice which word I put first)—then we will talk about the college search and application process in detail. But unless you've done your homework (literally and figuratively), you'll be limiting your choices unnecessarily.

You may get mixed messages from teachers, guidance counselors, other adults, your friends, and maybe even your parents when talking about the future. Even in middle school you'll start getting the question, "Where do you want to go to college?"

Here's the seemingly conflicting advice: "Don't grow up too quickly" and "But if you don't do well in school, you won't get into a 'good college.'"

Another variation might be: "You're only young once. Have fun" and "But if you don't take all honors courses and become president of your senior class, you can kiss Harvard good-bye."

Is there a reasonable middle ground here? You bet. *KickStart to College* will tell you how to have a good time, grow intellectually and emotionally, and, incidentally, how to get into the college of your choice. And as for Harvard? You can take every honors course your school has to offer and serve as president of your class all four years and you may or may not get into Harvard. It's more complicated than that (and I'll tell you why in this book).

The point of *KickStart to College* is to give you the information you need to gain more control of the college admissions process. There is a lot you can't do anything about, for example, geographic diversity: You live in New York City and want to go to a college in New England. Now, the last thing on earth any college in Boston needs is another kid from the Big Apple. But forget about it. You can't change where you live, the color of your skin, or where you went to high school. Get over it and move on. And you know what? That's exactly what the director of admissions at one Ivy League college told me. So let go of the stuff you can't control, and focus on the details you can control. (Actually that's not a bad lesson for life in general.)

KickStart to College will give you the information you need to plan your future. It's full of insider tips. Not only have I worked in the field for more than a dozen years and written several books on the topic, but most important, I have asked the people in charge the questions you would ask if you had the opportunity. I've quizzed them directly about what counts and what doesn't. I've pushed when their answers sounded like they were part of a public relations campaign rather than the truth. I've interviewed college admissions officers, athletic coaches, financial aid experts, alumni relations deans, teachers, parents, students, and, yes, lived through the process myself when my three sons were applying to college.

I began this book when my daughter was in the eighth grade. She was taking three accelerated high school classes, and I realized that these three grades would appear on her high school transcript. That reminded me that the college search process shouldn't begin in junior year of high school, but rather back in middle school when the choices are first being made.

When I said I was writing a college admissions book that began when the student was in the eighth grade, some people expressed concern. They said starting in the eighth grade was putting too much pressure on students at too early an age. I know eighth graders and high school freshmen and sophomores—people your age. I know you're smarter than that. You can take the information, use it wisely, and not get freaked out by it. In fact, that's my point. The more you know and the better educated you are about the process, the less pressure you will feel. You'll be in control of the process, rather than letting the process control you.

And where do parents fit into this process? In the interest of full disclosure, I am a parent, so I think it's important that the college planning process be a joint effort. But the truth is, you as the student will have to do all the heavy lifting, so to speak, and in the end, it has to be your choice. It is, quite simply, your life. Share this book with your parents. But more important, discuss your plans, hopes, dreams, and disappointments—about school, about your life—with them, too. Your parents come to the table with only your best interests at heart. They can be an incredible source of strength, have a perspective you will need, and be your best advocates as you navigate the tricky shoals that await you.

In the end, read and enjoy the journey—your journey.

Acknowledgments

I think I've wanted to write this book since my first son, Charles, was born … talk about planning ahead.

A few years later, my interest was piqued again when Charles was graduating from elementary school and planning his middle school schedule. There weren't many course choices, except for math. A group of students were selected to take an advanced math course. Because Charles was pretty strong in the subject, he was included, but several of his friends were not. They were smart kids, but they had never really applied themselves to their schoolwork—and who cared? They were only going into seventh grade. There would be plenty of time for them to get serious about school.

But here's what I learned: The decision about who would be admitted to that seventh-grade advanced math class determined who would take the AP math class, BC calculus, in twelfth grade. There was a tracking system for math, and it began in seventh grade! In fact, since the advanced math class in eighth grade was actually a course offered to ninth graders, that mark would appear on the high school transcript—the one that would be sent to colleges.

Hey, this was only middle school. How come we're talking about college already? And that's when I realized that what happens in middle school, and in ninth and tenth grade, count when you apply to college. Boy, did I have a lot to learn.

Well, I did. But more important, so did Charles, his brothers, Sam and Dan, and their sister, Maggie, who's in eighth grade right now.

Bottom line (I like to cut to the chase): Nobody wants a bunch of drudges who are only interested in grades. And by nobody I mean not your parents, not your teachers, and definitely not colleges. They all want to see students who are serious about education but who are also fun, interesting, and active in something. But you also do have to have good grades. How do you combine it all—and still have a good time in middle school and high school? You'll find out the details about what colleges want in the chapters ahead.

To write a detailed, practical college admissions guide, I needed more than my own personal experiences as the parent of applicants (three so far, one to go!). I worked for several years in the College Information Center (CIC) of our local high school. Hundreds of admissions representatives have come through the CIC, and I've learned a lot from their presentations and, even more important, from the pointed questions of guidance counselors and students who attended these sessions. I've researched this topic extensively and written other books on the subject, and I've also interviewed hundreds of people connected with the admissions process. These include college admissions directors at public and private, large, and small institutions; guidance counselors; private college admissions advisors; coaches on the high school and college levels; college alumni directors; teachers; financial aid experts; standardized testing experts; and of course, parents and students. Some were kind enough to speak on the record for attribution; others were willing to share their knowledge but asked for anonymity.

Special thanks to Willis J. Stetson, dean of admissions, University of Pennsylvania; Rory Shaffer-Walsh, director of admissions, Adelphi University; Michael Barron, director of admissions, University of Iowa; Carlton Surbeck, director of admissions, Goucher College; Ida Lawrence, Educational Testing Service; Jeff Rubenstein, assistant vice president for program development of The Princeton Review; Dr. Richard Bavaria, vice president of education for Sylvan Learning Centers; Mark Anestis, College Hill Coaching, Fairfield County, Connecticut; Eustace D. Theodore, eAdvancement.org, and immediate past president of the Council for the Advancement and Support of Education; Daniel White, eAdvancement.org; Ralph Polson, associate head soccer coach, College of Charleston; John Collins, swim coach for Olympic gold medalists; Robert Sweeney, counselor, Mamaroneck High School, and president of the Westchester/Rockland Guidance Counselors Association; Stephen Bauer, private college advisor; Carol B. Gill, private college advisor; Ann Kantor, guidance counselor, Hommocks Middle School; Trudy Hanmer, college advisor, Emma Willard School; Rebecca Peters, teacher, Emma Willard School; Robert Naeher, teacher, Emma Willard School; Robert Simms, teacher, Emma Willard School; John Cadwell, teacher, New Trier High School; Gerald Munley, teacher, New Trier High School; Lunetta Knowlton, former chair, music department, Mamaroneck High School; John Murray, AP art teacher, Mamaroneck High School; Lorna Minor, teacher, Mamaroneck High School; Barney Gill, teacher, Mamaroneck High School; Lorraine Henkel, teacher, New Rochelle High School; Marie Ruggiero, financial aid expert; Marlo Wiggans; Keith Wiggans; Thea Beaver; Bill Beaver; Alyssa Beaver; Kate Kelly Schweitzer; Aris Noah; Winnie Borden; Toni Walker Burke; Michelle LeCompte; Susan Gower; and Wendy Brooks.

Special thanks to my son, Sam Borden, whose patience, wit, and wisdom were especially helpful as I wrote this book. His insightful contributions enriched the chapters on athletic scholarships and campus visits. My heartfelt appreciation to my daughter, Maggie, whose good humor made the "deadline" weeks tolerable. Thanks, too, to Charles and Dan, both out of the house when this book was being written but who contributed to the general knowledge and whose encouragement was invaluable. As always, my love and gratitude to my husband, John. His unwavering support and love make it all possible.

The college application process can be tough, but it's also an opportunity to get to know what you want and plan for your future. I hope this book gives you back some of the control that is often lost as you go through the steps of applying to college. Good luck!

Chapter 1

Academics Plus

Coming Up in This Chapter

- Challenging yourself academically
- Knowing which grades count and why
- Finding the right help when you need it
- Realizing other academic options

Getting into the college of your choice will be the result of a combination of things: good grades, interesting extracurricular activities, excellent recommendations, powerful essays, strong standardized test scores—and luck. It's also a product of choosing the right schools for you so that admissions officers reading your applications say "This student belongs here."

In this chapter and the ones ahead, I'll talk about how you can take control, find a group of colleges that are right for you, and prepare effective applications for admission. First, the focus is on grades, the single most important ingredient of a college application.

Let's Get Organized: The College Box

Organization is the key to success—and to getting into college. As you begin your journey toward high school graduation and entry into college, it helps to have one place to put all the stuff you will accumulate over the next five years. It doesn't have to be fancy—a large cardboard file box, available at office supply stores, will do. You can even decorate it if you'd like.

This box, which I'll call your College Box, is the place where you will put the following:

- Copies of your report cards (if your parents want to keep the originals in their own files)
- Letters of commendation, honors, and awards you've won
- Newspaper articles about you
- Lists of your extracurricular and community service activities (updated each year)
- Sample essay topics you might use for your college application essays
- SAT and other standardized test scores
- Anything else related to the college topic, including interesting articles on higher education, college catalogues, and recruiting letters

You may decide to get even more organized and put the material in separate file folders. That's great, but at the very least, just put it all in one place so when you need the information, you'll know where to find it. It may be messy, but having one central place let's you know it's in there somewhere.

In every chapter, I'll tell you what materials you should be adding to your College Box.

Taking the Challenge

Let me state the obvious:

- The point of an education is to learn the material, not a score on a report card.
- It's to learn to think critically, not just to spit back memorized material.
- Getting straight A's doesn't necessarily make you an educated person, nor does an F in a course indicate that you aren't smart.

So trying your best and committing yourself to excellence is essential for becoming well educated. However, in the real world, your academic transcript is the most important part of your college application. And grades do count—even certain ones from eighth grade. Although middle school woodshop won't appear on your college transcript, your grade from your middle school French class may, because the grades from classes that are considered part of your high school curriculum will be included.

For example: In many school districts, students are required to take at least two years of a foreign language to graduate high school. While a student can start a language in seventh grade, the two years of middle school only count toward one year of completing the requirement (middle school foreign language classes are taught at a slower pace and use an entire year to cover a half-year's worth of material). Your grade from a foreign language class taken in eighth grade will appear on your high school transcript and will be factored in calculating your high school GPA and class rank.

And that's not the only mark from eighth grade that may appear on your transcript. Some schools permit advanced math students to accelerate in middle school and begin high school math in eighth grade. Those math marks appear on the high school transcript. So does the grade from the more advanced earth science course available to eighth graders.

Bottom line: Before you ever set foot in high school, you might already have three grades on your transcript that will be sent with your college applications. Sure, you'll have four years of high school grades to balance any problems you encountered in middle school, but those early grades can make a difference. For example, one high school senior regretted his casual attitude toward school in the eighth grade. He'd gotten his act together by tenth grade, but he missed being elected to the honor society in high school by one tenth of a point. Had his middle school grades been better, he would have been elected. This isn't earth-shattering, but it is unfortunate. Stay focused and serious in middle school—it can make a difference.

Choosing Your Courses

Over the next five years, you need to take the toughest course load you can carry. That's true no matter what college you want to go to. Again, back to the basics. You want to learn the material—that's what getting a good education is all about—and you want to grow and take all the intellectual challenges you can.

Every state has minimum requirements to graduate high school. These requirements outline the very least you need to do to get a high school diploma, although individual school districts and private schools may add additional requirements. Basically, you will need to take, from ninth grade through twelfth grade, courses in English, mathematics, science, and social studies. All states require students to take some physical education classes, although some districts give credit for participation in varsity level sports. Electives such as foreign languages, art, music, computer science, home economics, cooking, automobile shop, etc. round out the high school curriculum.

Bottom line: You can't hide or "fudge" your course choices. It's the job of a college admissions officer to know their applicants' high schools. If they don't have firsthand knowledge of the school, based on campus visits and years of experience, admissions officers have the profile or school description your counselor submits with your college application. This profile tells them what honors and AP classes are available in your school. They compare that list to your transcript. (We'll talk later about the issue of grades: Is it better to get an 85 in an honors or advanced placement course, rather than a 95 in a nonhonors class?)

English

Almost all states require at least four years of English in a combination of grammar, composition, and literature courses.

Bottom line: If you have the opportunity, go beyond the basics and include an elective English class to your schedule. Examining a subject and writing about it in a thoughtful, cogent way is essential in college. That's why college admissions officers take your application essay so seriously. It gives them a good clue about how well you will do in college classes. If your school offers them, in addition to the usual twelfth-grade English class, add a creative writing class or an extra literature course to your schedule. *It will be noticed.*

Independent Reading

No matter how heavy your academic course load may be, continue to read outside of school assignments. Jeff Rubenstein, assistant vice president for program development of The Princeton Review, points out that no amount of standardized test prep can equal the value of being a consistent reader. The vocabulary and language you learn just by reading gives you an edge both in taking standardized testing and in your regular coursework.

Unfortunately, one study points out that one third of American high school seniors don't read any books unless they are assigned school reading. Try to be in the other two-thirds.

Mathematics

Most states require at least three years of high school math. In addition to basic algebra, other courses might include higher-level algebra, geometry, trigonometry, math analysis or precalculus, calculus, statistics and/or probability, and computer science.

Math Around the World

According to the National Research Council, American students are sadly lacking in math skills. Our top 5 percent of math students is matched by the top 50 percent of students in Japan.

Bottom line: Even if you have always hated math, and even if every member of your family says they're no good at math, take advanced math classes throughout high school.

Noted mathematician John Allan Paulos points out that "There are differences in math ability, just like there are differences in literary ability. But people don't make the comparable arguments saying 'you're not going to be a journalist or novelist, so you might as well as forget the English courses.' They do tend to make that argument when it comes to mathematics."

Caution in Course Selection

Math classes tend to get tracked early. Check out your high school's requirement for honors classes as early as sixth grade, but certainly no later than eighth grade. In one school system, if you are not enrolled in the advanced math class in seventh grade, you won't be on track to begin the high school math program in eighth grade. This, in turn, automatically eliminates you from taking math honors classes in high school. You essentially make the decision about whether you will take an AP calculus class in twelfth grade when you're in sixth grade!

And despite the strides made in encouraging girls to pursue higher-level math courses, too often these classes are still male-dominated. Paulos finds, "Too often women will major in something they're not particularly interested in just to avoid a calculus or statistics requirement. Five years later they're earning one-half as much as the boy who sat next to them who was half as bright—but took math courses."

Math = $$$

In her book *Overcoming Math Anxiety*, Sheila Tobias points out that students who continue to take math classes throughout their educational careers can expect that their starting salaries will go up "$2,000 per year for every mathematics course taken after the ninth grade."

Sciences

Commonly, states require three years of high school science. In addition to biology, other science courses include physical science, earth science, chemistry, physics, botany, zoology, physiology, astronomy, applied physics, principles of technology, and qualified agricultural education courses (including horticulture, plant and soil science, natural resources and environmental science, and animal science).

Bottom line: It's more than Bunsen burners.

No matter whether you envision yourself as a scientist or not, consider taking advanced sciences classes throughout high school. These classes teach you much more than formulas and chemical equivalents. The lessons you learn are applicable to any subject area. From science classes you learn the following:

- To organize your thoughts
- To observe carefully
- To question the obvious
- To predict what *might* happen
- To test your predictions under controlled circumstances
- To make sense of results

Science Counts

One particular college wait-listed a strong student (that means she was put on list of students who may be admitted to the college if not enough accepted students choose to attend; see Chapter 10 for more). Her high school guidance counselor called the college and asked why. The college admissions officer admitted that it had bothered her that the student hadn't taken any AP science classes in her senior year. Instead, she had substituted additional dance and theater courses. The student eventually went to Yale.

Social Studies

Generally, three years of social studies courses are required. U.S. history is a prerequisite for all states, and schools may offer courses in world history, geography, economics, anthropology, as well as the specific state history.

Bottom line: Why study the past?

The analytical thinking, writing, and reading skills you need to study history will equip you for college—and for life. Taking history classes will help you understand the patterns of the past so you can understand the present and make sense of the future. Colleges expect you to take some history or social studies class in every year of high school.

Physical Education

All states have some phys ed requirement. Some require as little as a half year, but most require at least three years, if not all four years of high school. Some school districts permit you to substitute participation on a varsity level sports team for phys ed during the quarter that sport is in season.

The Arts and Other Electives

Most states understand that there is more to an education than just the three R's (reading, writing, and arithmetic) and require students to take courses in the visual arts and music as well. Many school districts also have foreign language requirements (usually a minimum of two years). Other elective subjects may include dance, video, automotive shop, or architectural drawing. Don't look just for academic subjects; choose electives that you enjoy.

One student who loved taking gourmet cooking classes in his high school found that his success in the kitchen translated into improved academic success. It takes organization and discipline to be a good cook—the same skills it takes to be a good student.

Bottom line: Say it in Spanish, French, Chinese, or any other spoken language. And don't forget to try some nonacademic subjects as well.

Most school districts require you to take at least two years of one foreign language. There are lots of good reasons to study a foreign language beyond the minimum requirements. In a study released by the New Jersey Department of Education, students who have had the opportunity to study a world language benefit in the following ways:

- Greater academic achievement in other areas of study, including reading, social studies, and mathematics.
- Higher scores on the Scholastic Achievement Test (SAT), American College Test (ACT), and other standardized tests, regardless of their ability level or socioeconomic status.
- Improved understanding of the English language and greater sensitivity to structure, vocabulary, and syntax.

- ☞ Improved reasoning, conceptualizing, and analyzing, along with better listening and memory skills.
- ☞ Enhanced employment opportunities and work relationships.
- ☞ Personal satisfaction through the ability to communicate across languages and cultures.

To gain the most benefit, study a foreign language for at least three years of high school.

Honors Classes

Your school may offer honors classes. These are courses in which the expectation is that students are ready for more challenging work than the mainstream classes. In honors classes you are expected to work fast and hard. You are expected to be self-motivated to do more advanced work. By taking the more challenging class, you are telling colleges that you understand the importance of working up to your potential as a student.

Your school may have prerequisites for admission to honors classes. These might include certain courses you need to have taken, a certain level of academic achievement in those classes, as well as teacher recommendations.

Advanced Placement Classes

Advanced Placement classes, or AP classes, are college-level studies that you can take while still in high school. Administered by the College Board, a nonprofit educational association that also administers the SATs, there are 35 courses in 19 subject areas available. But the number of courses given at individual high schools varies. AP teachers must meet certain criteria developed by the College Board. In May, you take an AP exam for each AP class in which you are enrolled (although you can choose not to submit your exam results to colleges if you are disappointed with the grades). AP exams are graded on a 1 to 5 scale, with 5 being the highest. Any 4 or 5 grade is excellent, and even a 3 indicates a solid performance in the course. Based on your performance, you can earn credit, advanced placement, or both, for college. Your score may earn you advanced placement credit. You could even enter college with enough credits to be considered a sophomore and finish your college coursework in three years. You are more likely to received advanced placement credit in state schools and less-competitive colleges.

But Harvard recently announced that it would only grant course credit for AP courses if you score a 5 on an AP exam, while the California Institute of Technology gives no advanced placement credit, regardless of your score. But for admissions purposes, the value of an AP class is that it shows colleges that you are ready to assume the challenge of a rigorous academic program.

In recent years, approximately 750,000 high school students around the globe took more than 1.25 million AP exams. Colleges use AP test results as part of their evaluation of applicants. According to the College Board, "Colleges and universities recognize that applicants with AP experience are much better prepared for the demands of college courses. Admissions officers are well aware of the difficulty of AP courses and exams, and sending them your AP exam grades can only be a positive step toward potential admission into competitive colleges." One study found that AP students are twice as likely to go into Ph.D. programs.

According to the College Board, "compared with regular high school courses, AP courses are usually more demanding. Depending on the subject, you may read and write more, analyze material, synthesize ideas, solve problems, and evaluate. Most AP classes are comparable to sophisticated college courses, so they aren't easy, but they're not impossibly difficult either."

What do you need to succeed in an AP class? According to the College Board, "you need to be willing and you need to be able. 'Willing' means motivated to study and learn on the college level. If you are committed to participating actively in an AP class and doing the out-of-class assignments, you have met a major prerequisite for success. 'Keeping up' is a basic practice for any college-level course. These courses move rapidly and cover a lot of ground. Successful students are those who keep up or, better, stay a little ahead of the required reading."

Selection criteria for AP classes are up to the individual high schools. Some schools have written guidelines for admitting students to AP classes. Generally, it's a combination of grades, teacher recommendations, and parent/student requests. Some schools permit any interested student to enter an AP class, while others limit participation.

Those schools with open AP course enrollment say that it gives every motivated student an opportunity to try a challenging academic program. If a student can't keep up, he can then transfer to a less-demanding course. The possible downside is that there may be scheduling problems if a student needs to leave an AP class. Some schools are concerned that by opening up the AP classes to any student who is interested, there will be a lower level of class discussion and a reduced number of students who do well on AP exams. But students who would normally be denied access to a course should be willing to argue that they are ready for the challenge, regardless of the grade.

If you change to a less-demanding class, talk to your counselor about what will appear on your transcript. You want to make sure it doesn't show the AP class (and grade), but only the mainstream class you complete. This shouldn't be a problem, because you will probably transfer by the end of the first quarter. But check your transcript to be sure.

Advanced Placement courses are now available in the following subjects:

- **Art:** four courses: Art History, Studio Art: Drawing Portfolio, Studio Art: 2-D Portfolio, and Studio Art: 3-D Portfolio
- **Biology:** one course
- **Calculus:** two courses: AB and BC
- **Chemistry:** one course
- **Computer Science:** A (this subject is the equivalent of a half-year college course) and AB
- **Economics:** Macroeconomics (this subject is the equivalent of a half-year college course) and Microeconomics (this subject is the equivalent of a half-year college course)

- **English:** three courses: Language and Composition, Literature and Composition, and International English Language (APIEL)
- **Environmental Science** (this subject is the equivalent of a half-year college course)
- **French:** two courses: Language and Literature
- **Geography:** Human Geography (this subject is the equivalent of a half-year college course)
- **German:** one course: Language
- **Government and Politics:** Comparative (this subject is the equivalent of a half-year college course) and United States (this subject is the equivalent of a half-year college course)
- **History:** three courses: European, United States, and World
- **Latin:** two courses: Literature and Virgil
- **Music:** Music Theory
- **Physics:** B, C: Electricity and Magnetism (this subject is the equivalent of a half-year college course), and Mechanics (this subject is the equivalent of a half-year college course)
- **Psychology** (this subject is the equivalent of a half-year college course)
- **Spanish:** two courses: Language and Literature
- **Statistics** (this subject is the equivalent of a half-year college course)

How Many AP Classes Should You Take?

This is never an easy question to answer. For admission to the most select schools, the more AP classes on your transcript—with good grades—the stronger your application.

At one elite private boarding school, the college counselor suggested that the strongest students graduate with seven or eight AP classes to their credit. That generally means they began taking AP classes in their junior year—perhaps even as early as their sophomore year. This kind of transcript might include two AP History classes (United States and European);

12

one English; one Foreign Language; two Sciences (Physics B in junior year and then another science AP in senior year); one or two Mathematics (one in junior year and a second in senior year); and perhaps an elective such as AP Art or Music, or Statistics or Computers.

The stress level for such an ambitious academic program would be intense—but for the Ivy League and other extremely selective colleges, you would probably need a minimum of four or five AP classes—with good grades and good AP scores—to be competitive for admission.

Bottom line: All colleges are impressed when you take even one AP class. It shows you are willing to take a challenge and you have developed good study skills that will prepare you for the rigors of college courses. It shows you have learned how to analyze problems, improved your writing skills, and learned how to prepare for college-level exams.

Appeals Court

But suppose you don't have all the necessary prerequisites for entrance into an honors or AP class, yet you want to take the more advanced class—what should you do? Is there an appeals process? Your school may have a regular method of dealing with students who have not been admitted to more advanced classes. If so, your guidance counselor can advise you. Take notes at each meeting so that you can explain to those further up the appeals process what has been said at a prior meeting.

If there is not a normal method of appeals, here's what to do:

1. Before you do anything, write your reasons for wanting to take the more difficult class, because, inevitably, you will have to make the case that you are qualified for the class. Writing your points will allow you to make a more persuasive, cogent argument.

   Realistically, no teacher wants to hear that your primary motivation for seeking placement in an advanced class is solely for improving your college application prospects. (Hopefully that isn't your primary reason, although it would be foolish to suggest that it is a not reasonable consideration.) Instead, the important buzzwords are that you "want a challenge" and "want to explore the subject in more depth."

If your academic record to date has been less than stellar, explain why you are ready now to take on an additional challenge (for example, you might point out that you are more mature now, that you recognize the importance and value of a challenging academic program, and perhaps that you've given up some of your extracurricular activities or a part-time job and have more time for your studies). As the College Board points out, "sometimes, students with quite mediocre records will blossom in a challenging classroom environment. The gain in student skills and confidence seems to counterbalance the lower average grades that may result."

2. After you have organized your arguments, talk to the department chair. Explain your reasons for wanting to enroll in the more difficult class. You might suggest that you can provide teacher recommendations (even if from an instructor in another subject) that will confirm your ability to do the work, as well as your commitment to excellence.

3. Talk to your guidance counselor and enlist her support. Ask her to speak to the department chair.

4. Offer to base your continued participation in the class on your first-quarter grades. You and your teacher should set a reasonable grade (for example, 80) and offer to withdraw if your first-quarter mark doesn't meet that agreed-upon grade.

5. If necessary, appeal to the principal of your school. Ask your parents to accompany you to the meeting, and follow up with a letter or e-mail that outlines what was said and the reasons given.

AP Exams Without the Classes

Technically, you can take an AP exam and submit it to colleges without taking the course in high school. Students for whom English is not their first language often take the AP exam of their native language. But if you are interested in taking an AP class and have been shut out either because the school won't admit you or because your schedule won't permit it, you can study the material on your own and take the exam in May.

One student was refused admission to her high school's AP American history class because of her low grades in earlier history classes. The student insisted that she was committed to learning the material and taking the class. She got the course material, studied on her own for the year, took the exam in May, and scored a respectable 3 (out of 5).

Other Academic Options

If your school won't admit you to honors classes or doesn't offer AP classes, consider enrolling in a local college while still attending high school. Without question, it will be demanding and expensive. You will attend regular high school, plus then attend evening classes at college. But going this route sends a very strong statement to the colleges to which you are applying. For example, one high school senior enrolled in a business class at a local college. Because he had indicated on his college applications that he planned to major in business, colleges were impressed that he had taken the initiative to pursue his interests even before graduating from high school.

In another example, one high school student found that she had completed all the advanced math classes in her school by the end of her junior year (she had accelerated the math program beginning in seventh grade when she was admitted to the eighth-grade advanced math class). Instead of just eliminating math from her courses during her senior year, she worked with her principal to find a long-distance learning program. Although she lived in New York, she enrolled online in an advanced math class given by Stanford University.

Grades: What They Do and Don't Tell You

You've been learning since the day you were born. But once you start elementary school, you begin getting evaluations on what you have learned. You may receive report cards with letter or number grades, or your school may give teacher-written evaluations with a narrative analysis of your performance in each subject.

Whether or not you agree with the need for grades, they are a part of the American educational system and can play a significant role in where you go to college. So the question is this: What do you do about your grades?

15

Some schools give letter grades, while others award number marks. The first table gives the numerical value of letter grades; the second table illustrates the numerical value of grade point averages.

Letter Grade	Numeric Value
A+	97 or above
A	93 to 96
A–	90 to 92
B+	87 to 89
B	83 to 86
B–	80 to 82
C+	77 to 79
C	73 to 76
C–	70 to 72
D+	67 to 69
D	65 to 66
F	Below 65, failing

Grade Point Average	Numeric Value
4.0	95
3.5	90
3.0	85
2.5	80
2.0	75
1.5	70
1.0	65
Below 1.0	Failing

First, remember, grades only tell you about past performance, that is, how much you accomplished in a subject over a specified period of time. They don't tell you about your short- or long-term academic future, so don't get freaked out if you receive a less-than-stellar grade—and don't get smug and complacent if you ace a certain subject.

Your report card should never be a surprise. You should be monitoring your performance throughout the marking period. If you are doing well, it's no time to slack off. If you are not doing well, as soon as you spot trouble, you should seek additional help. Although you may not be able to change the grade on any given test, you want to be sure and understand what you missed, so that you will be able to build upon that knowledge.

But it's sometimes possible to make up a bad test score—and you may not know that unless you ask. Here are some suggestions for making up points if you don't do as well as you'd like on a test:

- Sometimes a teacher allows a retest, especially if everyone in the class did poorly. One experienced teacher commented that "if half the students fail a test, then I didn't teach the subject well." So if you discover that many students fared poorly on an exam, you should ask the teacher about a make-up test. Some teachers will give a second examination and then average the two grades together.

- Ask about doing extra credit. Some teachers will give you the chance to improve your grades by doing extra subject-related projects. This is good insurance to take even if you are doing well in a class. One Spanish teacher gave students the opportunity to earn "gratis" during the marking period. In order to earn a gratis, the student had to participate actively in class and do some extra credit work, but for every 10 gratis earned, an extra point was added to the student's quiz average. The work was minimal, and the payoff was a nice bonus.

What If You Need Help?

If you are having trouble with a subject, you need to figure out what's going wrong. Not until you understand exactly what the problem is can you fix it.

First, look at the big picture. Is it a single subject you're struggling with (English? math?), or are you having problems with most of your schoolwork?

If it's a specific subject, then has this subject always been a problem for you, or is this something new? For example, do you usually do well in math, but lately have you been struggling with algebra? After you've figured that out, then get even more specific: Is it algebra or negative numbers? The more precise you can be about what you're having problems with, the easier it will be to tackle the problem.

If it's a broader problem, something that is affecting all your classes, then you need to know why. Ask yourself ...

- Is there a problem at home that's affecting your work (a parent's illness? divorce? loss of a job? relocation?)? Think about what is going on in your life and at home. Don't underestimate the pressures of change or stress. Ask your guidance counselor or a favorite teacher for an appointment to talk about what is happening and its effect on your schoolwork.

  Don't wait too long before asking for help. In fact, it is even better if you tell an adult at school when the crisis begins, rather than waiting to see if it has an effect on your schoolwork. It's a sign of maturity to ask for help, and your teachers would prefer to know and assist you before there is a serious problem, rather than play catch-up once your grades have begun to suffer.

  Although you may be hesitant to include your parents in this problem, especially if they are going through a difficult time in their own lives, they need to be involved. If you feel you can't approach your parents, ask your guidance counselor, a teacher, or someone in the school administration to intervene on your behalf.

- Have you taken a job? Working actually looks good on your college application. It shows you're a self-starter, takes initiative, and are well organized. But all in moderation. Researchers at Stanford and Temple universities found that students who worked more than 20 hours a week during the school year were more likely to ...

  - Have lower grades because they have less time to devote to their studies.

- Be more detached from their parents because they have less time to devote to family activities.
- Have a higher rate of alcohol and drug use because they have more discretionary income.

So if your grades begin to suffer, the first thing to evaluate is how many hours you are devoting to your job, including travel time. You may need a part-time job for financial reasons, but you may need to get help to balance long- and short-term goals. If the job helps pay for extras, such as your car or more expensive clothes, you need to rethink your priorities. On the other hand, if your family needs your earnings, then you may want to consider another job that will provide income but be less demanding in terms of hours and effort. Talk to your guidance counselor. She may be able to help you find a better, less-demanding job.

Remember: Good grades will help you get a good education, which in turn will help you earn more money in the long run.

- Did you begin a new activity? Get the lead role in a play? Play a sport and the season just start? You may need to reevaluate and reorganize your time. The answer is not necessarily to give up the extracurricular activity, but to see if there isn't some way to combine work and play. It may mean less TV or chat time on the computer or cutting back on hanging out with friends. But always remember that your first obligation is to your schoolwork.

- Is there a pattern in your grades? You may need to go back and check your academic performance for a few years to see if the grade slippage has happened before under similar circumstances. For example, one student often had problems during the third quarter of every year. Maybe it was because he kept it together for a half year and then lost steam. He generally rebounded in the fourth quarter—but forewarned is forearmed. He learned to be aware of his tendencies and, as soon as the pattern emerged, to take steps on his own to work smarter.

Where to Get Help

If you're having a problem with a subject—math, English, history, science—you may need to find a tutor. You can begin at home—your parents or an older sibling may be able to supplement the classroom instruction. Sometimes it's just a matter of reviewing the material and putting the technical terms into layman's terms. Or it could just be that the pace of the classroom instruction is too fast, and with a little more time and effort, you can catch up on your own.

But if working with your relatives is adding too much stress to family relationships, you may want to seek outside assistance.

Begin with your teacher. Every classroom teacher should be available either before school, during lunchtime, or after school for extra help. If your teacher hasn't already announced her "office" hours, ask about it. Make an appointment, and if necessary, get the requisite hall pass or whatever permissions are necessary to come before or after school.

Don't be embarrassed to ask for help—even if you have to go every single day for additional tutoring. Helping you learn is your teacher's job.

If you find that you are still having problems (which can certainly happen if your teacher isn't particularly good at explaining the subject matter), you may want to consider getting outside help. Here are some suggestions for finding the help you need.

Study Groups

Study groups are common in college but can be an effective way of learning in middle and high school, as well. They are a way of sharing and expanding the information you need to learn for a course, especially when there is a great deal of material to be covered. Study groups are also helpful in presenting different perspectives on the course material. But to be effective, all members of the group have to be equally committed and organized. You may decide to meet on a weekly basis throughout the semester or choose to meet several times just prior to exams. Here are the basics:

1. Keep the group small, between three and six members. It can work with just two of you, but with a slightly larger group, even if one person can't make the meeting, the rest of you can still carry on.

2. Make sure all members are on about the same level of expertise. There's a difference between a tutorial—where one person consistently teaches the material—and a study group, where you are all sharing information. Although at different points during the course, one member of the group may, in fact, end up as "teacher." If this is consistently one person's role, she may not feel that the study group is worth the investment of her time.

3. One person should serve as chair of the group, scheduling the meetings and making sure you stay on topic. Keep the chit-chat during the meeting to a minimum (members can stay afterward if they want to socialize). If your group meets just to prepare for exams, the chair should assign the material each person is to cover by phone or e-mail so the group can begin reviewing material at each meeting, rather than needing to spend time organizing the mechanics of the group.

4. At the end of each meeting, set the agenda for the next session. Assign each member of the group a section of the material for which they are responsible. They will report on that section, and prior to an exam, prepare sample questions and answers. Divide the work evenly among the members.

5. Limit the study sessions to one to two hours—more than that is counterproductive. Each person should present the material he prepared, then open the session to discussion and questions. Each member should bring copies of the material he prepared so that each member of the group can use it as a study aid.

If You Need a Private Tutor

If you need additional help, your first stop should be your teacher. But if you find that you are still having problems and need one-on-one help, you may want to consider hiring a private tutor. You will want someone who not only knows the material, but can communicate it well. We all know math whizzes who have trouble putting a noun and verb together in the same sentence. Teaching is an art and a science.

To find an effective tutor …

- Check your school's honor society. Some offer peer tutoring for free.
- Some school districts maintain a list of student volunteers who will help their peers or younger students for free. Other schools have youth employment services where students willing to tutor can register. You will probably have to pay, but it's probably considerably cheaper than an adult tutor.
- Check the employment offices at local colleges for students willing to tutor.
- Ask your guidance counselor. He may be able to recommend retired teachers who are willing to tutor. Posting a help wanted card at the senior center could also put you in touch with someone who knows the topic. The person may not have taught, but again, he might be someone who worked in the field, understands the subject, and can communicate well.
- A great website for finding one-on-one tutoring is www.tutor.com. This online service provides tutoring for libraries, community-based organizations, schools, companies, publishers, and individual students. For as little as $20 an hour, you get access to qualified tutors for live instruction. Help is available in all subjects for grades kindergarten through 12 and includes tutoring for Advanced Placement classes.

Before hiring a tutor …

- Check references. You want to ask previous customers if the tutor knows the topic and can communicate well.
- Review the material that needs to be covered. Establish whether you will meet on a regularly scheduled basis or just before exams.
- Work out the logistics such as where will you meet and how often. Be on time and be prepared for each session.
- Agree on a price. Expect to pay between $6 and $10 per hour for a high school student and as much as $35 to $75 per hour for an experienced teacher.

Do You Have a Learning Disability?

Your failing grades may be symptomatic of a bigger problem. If school-work has always been difficult for you, you may have an undiagnosed learning disability. Not all learning disabilities can be easily detected. You may have been compensating for your learning problems by working harder. You may have been struggling since grade school, never quite understanding why it was so much harder for you to learn than for your classmates. But now that you are entering high school, where the academic demands are so much tougher, it's more important than ever to get the help you need.

Learning disabilities are defined as lifelong, neurologically based conditions that interfere with a person's ability to store, process, and retrieve information. While it sounds scary, many successful adults have learned to compensate for their disabilities. George Bush, former president and father of the current president, is dyslexic and has difficulty reading. It's estimated that 15 to 20 percent of the U.S. population has some learning disability. Learning disabilities often run in families, so if your parents or siblings have had difficulty learning, be sure and share that information with your teacher.

The National Center for Learning Disabilities has developed a checklist of common warning signs of learning disabilities. All kids have some of these behaviors at one time or another, so don't get worried if you recognize one or two of the signs in yourself. A *consistent* display of a *group* of these behaviors is the tip-off that you might want to talk to a specialist. Check out their website at www.ncld.org.

Learning Disabilities and Academic Success

If you suspect you have a learning disability, even if it has not been diagnosed until now, you will need to get evaluated by professionals. Talk to your parents about getting tested. Your family doctor, teachers, and guidance counselor are all good resources for finding help.

Bottom line: If you have been diagnosed with a learning disability, or suspect you have one, you need to talk to your parents and seek help.

Learning disabilities may make your schoolwork more difficult, but you can be taught how to compensate for your problems. With the right assistance, your college dreams can be realized.

Weighted Grades

Some schools choose to weight the grades for honors and AP classes. That means extra grade points are awarded to students in those classes. The amount of weighting is solely dependent on the school district, and some schools choose not to weight grades at all. About half the high schools in the nation weight their grades.

For example, in Kankakee, Illinois, "weighted grades will be used to determine the honor roll, class valedictorian, and academic awards, as well as rank in class." The school district attaches an explanation of their weighting system to students' transcripts. Weighted grades are given for courses that are academic (that is, not phys ed classes) and are college-preparatory. The Kankakee school district weights advanced courses in English, math, and the sciences and "courses which are clearly more demanding than those courses taken by students who are not college-bound." This school district's weighting system is as follows:

Regular Courses	College Prep Courses*	Honors Courses**
A = 4.0	A = 4.5	A = 5.0
B = 3.0	B = 3.5	B = 4.0
C = 2.0	C = 2.5	C = 3.0
D = 1.0	D = 1.5	D = 2.0
F = 0	F = 0	F = 0

College prep courses are designed for students who have made a commitment to a four-year program of studies in the college prep curriculum.
**Honors courses are limited to students who have a B average and are in the upper 15 percent of their class.*

In this high school, the valedictorian is the student who not only has a straight-A average, but who has taken the maximum number of honors courses.

But there isn't any consistency among schools as to which classes are weighted, which grades are affected (some schools choose not to inflate all grades or only the grades received in the senior year), nor how transcripts are marked to indicate school policy. This last point is important, because many colleges reconfigure grade point averages if they know that the school weights their grades. However, realistically, this doesn't always happen. With the average college application only receiving a 10-minute scrutiny, it's hard for the admissions officer to recalculate each applicant's average.

Generally, weighted grading policies use a 5.0 instead of a 4.0 scale. A student who excels and has taken a heavy load of honors and AP classes could easily end up with a grade point average that exceeds 4.0, the generally accepted standard of academic perfection.

The reasoning behind the no-weighted-grades policy is a basic assumption that there is no reason to reward students who are enrolled in advanced classes because they are just doing the work they are prepared to do. In other words, if a student is in a regular class, the presumption is that he has taken the most challenging program he can. Therefore, his grade in the class should not be "discounted" because he didn't take an honors or AP course. Conversely, the honors student has also taken a class that matches his ability, so his grade should not be inflated because he is doing work he is prepared to do.

But advocates for weighted grades suggest that it encourages students to take the most demanding classes and not worry that their averages will suffer because they've accepted a challenge. Furthermore, when competing for scholarships and college admission, nonweighted grades may put students at a disadvantage when pitted against students from schools that do weight their grades. Finally, there is a frustration among students when the valedictorian of the class is someone with the highest grades but who did not take the most demanding coursework.

Students see their class ranking in a school with nonweighted grade policies as slipping because it's based on just a straight numerical average rather than a reflection of the challenges taken and met. As reported in *Education Week*, one student who had taken honors English and received a

B for his efforts complained that "There are a few people above me in rank who haven't taken honors courses. They just don't want to work. I could easily have gotten A's in regular English."

Because each school district develops their own rules regarding weighting, some choose not to weight grades a student receives from another school. This can mean that the student who enrolls in classes at a local college while still in high school may have the grade included on his transcript but not reflected in his grade point average or not weighted as other high school grades would be. In one Colorado high school, the salutatorian lost the valedictorian spot by less than one-hundredth of a point because, having fulfilled her high school academic requirements, she took college classes in the second half of her senior year at a local university. Those grades were not weighted, so she ceded the number-one position in the school—a post she had previously held for three and a half years of high school.

Similarly, one student moving after tenth grade from a Maryland school district that weighted grades to a North Carolina high school that did not found his grade point average plummeting. In ninth and tenth grade he had challenged himself with classes in the gifted and talented/Advanced Placement level. He had received A's, B's, and C's, but a B in this program was equal to a 4.0 instead of the nonweighted 3.0. However, the North Carolina school only recorded the grade—not the weighting that the district would have used when computing class rank. Moreover, even if the school district had weighted grades, they might have decided only to weight those for which there was a comparable class in both districts. If Maryland offered an honors music class but North Carolina did not, there would be no designation of honors on the transcript.

Finally, there is unofficial weighting. Even in school districts that don't weight grades, some teachers may choose to do so. One honors math teacher announced at the beginning of the year that he would add two points to the quarterly grades of those students who did their homework and actively participated in class. He believed that students should be rewarded for taking the more challenging class. Another variation was the AP Computer Science teacher who took the square root of a student's quarterly average and multiplied it by 10 for the final grade of the quarter. This teacher didn't weight grades in any of her regular classes, nor did she ever round up a grade—an 84.7 grade was an 84. But she believed that her method of grading in the AP class was realistic and appropriate for such a challenging college-level class—and one that would be duplicated if the student had taken the class in college.

Bottom line:

- Although your overall grade point average is important, which classes you take are even more important. College admissions officers will notice that you took more challenging classes, even if the grades are not as high and have not been weighted.

- Understand what the rules are at the beginning. Find out whether your school district has a weighted grade policy. Also, if a teacher doesn't explain his grading policy at the beginning of the school year, ask if he gives any extra credit for taking an honors class.

Which Is Better?

One high school student asked the admissions officer of an Ivy League university, "Which is better, an 85 in an honors class or a 95 in a regular class?"

Without missing a beat, the admissions officer coolly answered, "A 95 in an honors class."

Obviously, it's best to get great grades in whatever class you take, and that will take hard work and commitment. But this same admissions officer, like every other one interviewed, says flatly, he is more impressed with the difficulty of courses taken.

If you are really tanking in an honors class, it's time to consider transferring to a regular class. But if it's a question of a grade in the 80s in an honors class versus topping the charts in a regular course, take the challenge.

One experienced math teacher wrote in his recommendation letter for a student, "I admire this student because he willingly took the challenge of the more demanding math class. While he could have gotten great grades in the regular program, I encouraged him to take this AP class. His quarterly grade is only an 80, but his motivation to learn is great, and his attitude toward academic challenges is what every college hopes to see." The student was admitted to a top-ranked university.

Add to Your College Box

- Keep copies of all academic records and report cards (quarterly as well as year-end). You will want to compare the transcript the guidance counselor will send with your college applications to the records you have been maintaining. Calculate your own GPA, and, if necessary, ask questions if there is a discrepancy.

- Store any term papers or essays from junior year on for which you received a grade above a 90 or an A. Some schools want to see a writing sample of an academic paper, and you may be able to use one of these.

- Keep any essays that might be used for personal statements requested by colleges.

- Include any letters of commendation for academic achievement, as well as notices that you have made the honor roll or been accepted for membership in the honor society.

What You Need to Know

- Your academic record, including some middle school courses, are the most important part of your college application.

- If you need help in a class, don't wait to get it—the sooner the better. Asking for help is a sign of maturity.

- Push yourself to take the most challenging academic courses you can. You should do this because it gives you the best education, as well as strengthens your college application.

Chapter 2

Sport Smarts

Coming Up in This Chapter

- Are sports in your college future?
- Getting started in sports in middle school
- Using athletics to get into college
- The tough world of college athletics—are you ready?

There's no reason why your love of sports can't be an asset when applying to college—in fact, it could even pay for it! Look, you shouldn't devote hours to a varsity team or amateur sports program unless you enjoy it. But if you love sports and if you are ready to commit the time and energy necessary, this chapter will tell you what you need to know to use your middle school/high school athletic career to your advantage.

Whether or not you hope to play in college, your active participation in a sports program will tell colleges a lot about you. No matter what level you play—junior varsity, varsity, elite, or just intramurals—colleges will see that you know how to manage your time well, that you can balance academic and outside demands, and that you can work as part of a team. These skills are also important components of a successful college academic career and also reveal that you enjoy making a contribution to your community.

Beginning a Sports Career

If you love all sports—or just one sport in particular—you've probably been playing for years. In many towns Little League starts in kindergarten, kids strap on hockey skates almost as soon as they learn to walk, swimmers compete in meets by age six. Elite travel teams, essentially the best players in the area, are often established by age eight—with intense tryouts for spots on the team. Each year, the competition to remain on the select team may be more difficult and the inter-team contests more formidable.

Middle school teams are essentially the farm system for high school junior varsity and varsity sports. But whether or not you can play on your middle school's team depends on your skill and the district's policies. In some schools, anyone who wants to play can find a spot on the team. Because of this no-cut policy, some team rosters are huge. This plus your ability will make a difference in the amount of playing time you'll probably get. If you're a strong competitor, you may be frustrated because in these types of inclusive programs, all team members will see some time on the field regardless of ability. For less-competitive players, the advantage of this type of team is that all you need to do to play is show up for all practices and make an effort.

In other school districts, middle school teams are competitive from the get-go. You have to earn your place on the team, fight to keep it, and prove again and again your ability and value to the team.

Bottom line: Before the season begins, you need to find out …

- What the policies are in your school district.
- Who the team coaches are and what their coaching philosophies are.
- Whether the teams are competitive or primarily skills clinics.
- If there is a regular playing season against other schools or if you will be playing against other teams from your own school.

Learning to Play the Game

In one town, there were recreational opportunities to play baseball, softball, hockey, basketball, football, soccer, and lacrosse, as well as a competitive swimming program. But there weren't any recreational field hockey or fencing programs—although the high school had varsity teams for both sports. Middle school was the place where students first learned skills for these sports. The seventh-grade field hockey and fencing teams were essentially skill clinics. Eighth graders entered competitive play against teams from other area schools. By ninth grade, when they entered high school, students could join the freshman team or, if they were exceptionally talented, move on to the junior varsity level. A student's decision to join a middle school team was critical to his being able to play in high school, because that's where he first learned to play the game.

Jumping the Gun

Exceptional middle school athletes may be permitted to play on high school teams. This can be good if you are a student who is ready for a higher level of competition, and it also extends your athletic career, allowing you to play more than just the four years of high school. But there's a downside to this. You will be playing with kids who are older and more experienced than you. Part of being a member of the team is making friends and being part of a social group. You may feel awkward hanging out with kids who can be up to five years older than you. Furthermore, in some states, once you have passed the various tests necessary to join the high school teams and have been accepted as a member, you can't return to the modified middle school program. If it doesn't work out on the varsity level, you may end up having to sit out the season completely.

Skipping middle school teams in favor of high school athletic programs is really intended for kids who are physiologically mature, physically fit, and athletically gifted. Even if you are the star of the middle school football team, it doesn't mean that you are ready to forego eighth-grade competition. You will have an opportunity to shine later on. Playing up is a step that should be carefully considered.

You will have to check with your coach or your school district's athletic director about what the district regulations are concerning student participation on athletic teams beyond their grade placement. For some, a coaching staff recommendation is all that is required. In others, not only do you need the coaching staff recommendation, but you also have to pass a physical fitness test that even many gifted athletes would find difficult to pass. To participate in a higher-level athletic team in New York State, a student needs ...

- ✐ To get parental permission.
- ✐ An assessment by a member of the middle school physical education staff who knows him.
- ✐ Medical approval.
- ✐ To pass an arduous physical fitness test.
- ✐ To have his athletic skills evaluated by the coach of the high school team.

Is a Team Important?

If you want to be a basketball player, odds are your high school has varsity, junior varsity (JV), and even modified teams, and they probably even have an intramural program for the students who don't make the cut. But suppose your sport doesn't have a school-sponsored team? You will need to pursue your interests on your own. For example, if you are a figure skater, you will need to find ice time for practice, personal coaches and choreographers, and costumers, and figure out how to carve out countless hours for practice before and after school. You will have to travel to participate in U.S. Figure Skating Association competitions, and you will want to get regionally and nationally ranked. But colleges are impressed by a student's efforts to pursue her passions and note when it takes more effort than just showing up after school for a team practice.

Bottom line: You want to excel at sports, and to be recruited by a college athletic program you need to play at the highest level of competition you can find. That said, consider carefully before you accelerate your athletic career in middle school. Playing as part of a team of your peers is part of the fun of school. Enjoy that time.

Nontraditional Sports

Never join a sport because it will get you into college. That goes without saying. But if you can become exceptionally good in high school in a sport that is generally not available to high school students, for example, fencing, crew (especially girl's crew), and girl's hockey, it might give you an edge in your college selection process.

Your high school may not field teams in these sports, so you may have to go to a larger community and join a program there. That probably means an investment of time and money, but to become competitive in these sports can be a real plus.

Benchwarmer with Style

You've made the high school team, but you have seen a total of maybe five minutes of play. Are you supposed to be like Rudy Ruettiger, who was featured in the 1993 film *Rudy*, who so worshipped Notre Dame University football that he spent nine years and overcame incredible obstacles to join the team? He actually played only 27 seconds in his entire college career. Is there a value to being on the practice squad—the ones whose job it is to make the "real" players look better?

That depends. Any sport takes a lot of time, and only you can decide if the role you will play on a team makes it worthwhile. If you think it is, enjoy playing and even consider writing your college essay about what being part of a team has taught you. In fact, that's a better essay than describing how you felt scoring the winning touchdown (see Chapter 7 on writing college essays). One undistinguished member of a high school track team began his essay by saying "I'm no Carl Lewis [an Olympic gold medalist]. In fact, I couldn't beat Carl Lewis's dog in a track meet. But I love being on the track team." Then he proceeded to describe his experiences. The self-awareness of this applicant must have made a good impression on colleges—he got into six of the eight schools to which he applied.

But there's a flip side. If you don't think you'll be satisfied being a benchwarmer or playing a minimum amount of time, maybe it's time to reconsider your participation. No one is looking for a quitter or a spoil-sport, but there are other activities, and you might want to give them a try. One ninth grader was devastated when he was cut from the high school basketball team. Under duress he joined the fencing team, and, after three years on the high school team, he was recruited by colleges impressed with his fencing accomplishments.

Bottom line: If you love your sport and are willing to be part of it in any way possible, be a proud benchwarmer. But if sitting on the sidelines doesn't work for you, consider moving on and spending your time in more productive ways.

Investing in Sports

If you hope to play sports in college, you will definitely have to invest some time and money. You will need to play on elite teams and be seen by college coaches, but you will also have to attend summer programs and seek outside coaching to improve your skills. As Ralph Polson, associate head soccer coach at the College of Charleston, points out, "everyone who plays on a college team has been the star of their high school team." That alone isn't enough. What else have you done? Polson says he needs to see that the player has been on select teams, has attended summer skills camps, and, preferably, has been part of the Junior Olympic Development program. (Most Olympic sports sponsor programs to develop young talent. Check the website of the national accrediting organization of your sport to find out if there is an affiliated Junior Olympics Development program.)

For certain sports, you will need to get ranked by participating in local, state, and then national meets sponsored by the supervising athletic association. One student with average grades strengthened his college application because he was ranked fourteenth in the nation in archery. Obviously, it limited the schools to which he could apply if he hoped that the archery would make a difference. But he wanted to continue the sport in college and chose a school in Arizona that wanted him both as a student and as a member of the archery team.

College Recruiting

Let's be honest. You're reading this next part of the chapter because you're the captain of the soccer team, or the leading scorer on the basketball team, or the number-one goalie on the hockey team and you think you'd like to play while you're in college, right? Along with classes and dorms, you're hoping that seeing yourself on ESPN every third night will be a regular part of your collegiate experience.

Okay, now here's the honesty part: Even if you're not a math major, you'll quickly realize that the odds of this happening are stacked against you.

As an example, the National Collegiate Athletic Association (NCAA— or "the Almighty" if you actually do make a team) estimates that there are roughly 550,000 male basketball players in high schools across the country. Only about 15,700 of them will ever make a college basketball team. That works out to only about 3 percent of the players who dominated their county tournaments and set records in their local leagues getting to even put on a jersey at one point or another. Of course, it's worth noting that a lot less of that 3 percent will ever see themselves on *SportsCenter,* because Stuart Scott rarely goes "Boo-yah!" for a jump shot by someone on the Emory University hoops squad, or on any of the other Division-III schools.

So consider yourself warned. College recruiting is a brutal process, mostly because of the limited amount of spaces available each year. In economics terms, supply is far outweighed by demand. In simple terms, it's pretty darn hard.

Some Quick Definitions

One of the most difficult parts of understanding college athletics is figuring out exactly what everything means. The NCAA sanctions teams in three divisions—easily enough named Division I, Division II, and Division III—but each of them has different rules about what a college must do to qualify for play in that particular division.

Division-I (D-I) schools are the big ones, like the University of Florida or the University of Michigan. They are the ones that you see on television each weekend, playing in front of huge crowds in mammoth stadiums. They are the big time in college athletics. There are lots of smaller criteria for defining Division-I programs, but it's all pretty mundane. The most basic of these requirements is that the school has to sponsor at least seven sports for men and seven for women (or six and eight, as long as the eight is for women).

For schools that have football (and no, not every Division-I school must have football), the NCAA requires a certain minimum attendance at games for the school to be classified as Division I. If a school does not want to (or can't) meet the attendance requirements, it can be classified as Division I-AA in football only.

Division-I schools are also responsible for meeting minimum financial aid awards for their athletes (this is where the scholarships, also known as "rides," come in), but they are bound by maximum financial aid requirements as well. The NCAA sets the minimum and maximum number of scholarships that must be met for each team. The Ivy League is the lone exception to this rule, because there are no athletic scholarships available at Brown, Columbia, Cornell, Dartmouth, Harvard, Penn, Princeton, and Yale.

Division II (D-II), like Southwestern Oklahoma State University in Weathersford or St. Michael's College in Colchester, Vermont, schools are much different than their D-I brethren. They are similar in that scholarships are allowed, but it is rare for students to get full scholarships from the athletic department since D-II athletic programs are financed in the school's budget like any other academic department on campus. More frequently, D-II athletes will get a partial scholarship and pay for the rest of their costs through grants, loans, and work-study earnings. D-II schools are defined by certain scheduling restrictions and are a great opportunity for top-notch local and regional athletes who may not be able to make their way on to the teams at the D-I level.

Division-III (D-III) schools, like Trinity College in Hartford or the University of California San Diego, are where student-athletes play for the love of the game and little else. Crowds can be small at these schools, and the university treats the athletic program just like every other department. There are no athletic scholarships available and coaches have limited recruiting budgets. But despite these restrictions, the competition at D-III schools is fierce. There are a number of storied rivalries, particularly among small local schools. Williams and Amherst wage a football battle each fall that draws thousands of fans, and there is a purity about D-III athletics that makes it particularly appealing. If you are a great power forward—but plan on being an even better lawyer—a Division-III school may be the best decision you can make.

Getting Started

Coaches will always tell you that the best way to prepare for a tough opponent is to make sure that *you* are 100 percent ready to play. There's a similar line of thinking when it comes to getting yourself noticed by college coaches, because it's impossible for you to know what the thousands of other high school hopefuls are doing—you have to concentrate on yourself.

If you think that you might want to play sports in college, one of the best things you can do is make sure that your games are being videotaped. Videotapes are one of the best ways for coaches on limited travel budgets (as most small D-I, D-II, and D-III coaches are) to weed out the players that most interest them without having to leave campus. If you go to a high school that doesn't routinely record its varsity games, maybe you or your parents could invest in a video camera and tape your own games. But be smart about how you tape your games; a coach can't tell anything about how talented you are if he only sees *you*, so don't bother sending a

"Jimmy's Greatest Hits" (or "Jimmy's Greatest Goals" or "Jimmy's Greatest Saves"). If you can, ask a friend or family member—or maybe even hire someone—to tape the whole game so the college coach can see you perform in the context of an entire game.

And don't be afraid to make contact with coaches early. If you've got your heart set on a particular school, send the coach a letter when you're a freshman, telling him you're going to work as hard as you can over the next four years to make yourself attractive to his program. If you've got a particularly good tape, send that as well. What's the worst that can happen? There are few coaches anywhere who don't admire determination and perseverance, so don't be afraid to get in touch. (See the sample letters later in this chapter.)

It doesn't pay to be picky early in your high school career. If you think you might be interested in a school, establish a line of communication with the coach there. You never know where your paths will cross—coaches often work at summer camps, using them as an opportunity to check out prospective talent—and so any edge that might make you stand out from the pack is worthwhile.

What Does It Take?

There are no set requirements to be a college athlete. Not everyone was the captain of their high school team, and not everyone played in the Junior Olympics. Those things don't hurt, of course, but they certainly aren't necessary. The reality is that it comes down to an evaluation of talent—whether or not a coach thinks you possess the talent, or the potential, to help his team be a winner.

But as a high school student, the best thing you can do to make yourself attractive to a college coach is to challenge yourself on a consistent basis. Obviously, depending on where you live and what competition is available to you, that means different things. If you play a team sport and there is a Junior Olympic Development Program available in your area, you would certainly want to try and get on it. If you play an individual sport and you need to travel during the summer to find better competition, that is something you should certainly consider. This isn't to suggest that statistics don't matter—of course a coach will want to know your batting average, your scoring average, or your save percentage—but coaches will also want to know the relative value of those numbers and whether they were easy or hard for you to attain.

Bottom line: The key is to look around your city, your state, and your region and ask yourself "Where are the best players playing?" and then go play against them. If you play on a club soccer team that switches leagues to play against easier competition, you might want to look into changing teams, so you will be able to keep competing against the strongest competition. Then, if you succeed, you know (and more important, the college coach will know) that you are more than just an athlete who looks good "on paper."

Letters

Letters are the primary way for student-athletes to correspond with college coaches, and much of the initial contact is through the mail. The student sends an introductory letter, and the coach responds with a brochure or a packet that outlines what being an athlete at his school is like. The student sends an update letter to let the coach know how a season is going, and the coach responds with a similar piece, keeping the student up to date as to how the program is doing. This dialog is very important for both the student and the coach, because it sets the groundwork for any recruiting relationship that will exist when the student gets closer to making his college choices.

The most important thing about your letters, though, is to not be afraid of being egotistical. You are trying to sell yourself, and to do that you can't be afraid to point out your qualities. Equally important, however, is giving some meaning to what you write. If, for example, you write about how your soccer team won the Sun Bowl tournament over Christmas break, tell the coach who the competition was—and if you were the MVP, tell him why.

Name-dropping can be important in these letters as well. If you play on a team that is coached by a college coach or an otherwise noteworthy person, put that person's name in your letter. If you've gone to a camp where a professional evaluated you, put that person's name in your letter. You don't want to go overboard—your letter shouldn't look like the *Who's Who*—but if recognizable names will lend credence to your product (which, in this case, is you), then by all means you should mention them.

Once you've established contact with a coach, sending follow-up letters to keep him abreast of the things you're doing is the next step. These days, e-mails are easier (and cheaper) to send, and if a coach doesn't have a problem corresponding electronically, you may want to stay in touch with him that way. Regardless of the form it takes, update letters are just that: a chance to tell the coach that you're maintaining (or better, improving) your skills, working hard, and continuing to challenge yourself. In these letters you can let him know what awards you've won or tournaments you've played in. If you're going to a camp or playing a game near the coach's university, give him the date and time and tell him that you would love to have the chance to be evaluated.

Sample Letters to a College Coach

Following are letters sent by John Jones, a high school student, to a Coach Smith at a Division-I school. A soccer goalkeeper, John was determined to play at a Division-I school. The names have been changed for privacy purposes, but the information is accurate. It's worth noting that John did end up being recruited to play for a Division-I school, but not for Coach Smith.

Sent November of John's junior year of high school:

Dear Coach Smith:

Based on research I am doing in preparation for choosing a college, Super College has an excellent reputation in both academics and athletics.

The enclosed resumé details my academic standing and soccer experience. I am currently a junior at Beacon High School with a GPA of 3.3 on a 4.0 scale, and I am taking honors college preparatory classes. Super College offers a variety of degree plans that interest me, although I have not yet decided on a specific major area of study.

I would work hard to continue to develop my skills and abilities as a goalkeeper in a Division-I program, and I would like to continue to develop my soccer talents under your style of play. I will be playing with my club team, the Cavaliers, in the Georgia Open Cup at the Lovejoy Fields in Fayetteville, Georgia, beginning November 21, in the Charleston Thanksgiving Soccer Shootout, and in the Tampa Sun Bowl over Christmas.

Thank you for any consideration you can give me. Please send me information on your program as well as any suggestions you have on how best to prepare to attend Super College in the fall of 2000.

Sincerely,

John Jones

Follow-up letter sent two months later:

Dear Coach Smith,

Just a quick note since I wrote to you in November to update my soccer activities. My club team, the Cavaliers, won the under-18 division of the Charleston Thanksgiving Soccer Shootout, and I was named the division's Most Valuable Player. Unfortunately, we did not fare as well in the Tampa Sun Bowl over Christmas. We did not advance out of our bracket, but we were the only team to not lose to the champion of our under-18 division as we tied the Tulsa Thunder 2–2.

I am looking forward to high school soccer starting in a few weeks as soon as I finish the varsity basketball season where I am currently the starting point guard. Please know that I am still interested in a goalkeeper position at Super College, and I appreciate the correspondence you have sent me. Please let me know if there is any further information I can provide to you.

Sincerely,

John Jones

Letter written at the end of junior year:

Dear Coach Smith,

Since writing to you in the fall and then again after Christmas, I thought I should update you on my spring's activities and on my plans for the next few months. My high school team had a record of 12–5–1, and we were state runner-up in the A/AA division after losing to five-time champion St. Pius 2–1. I was voted Most Valuable Player by my teammates and was also named the first team goalkeeper on the All Northeast Georgia Soccer Team for the second year.

I have recently changed club teams, and I am now the goalkeeper on the under-18 Knights Sporting FC with Joseph Jackson as my coach. We are in the Super Group and will be playing in the tournaments in Memphis in August, Houston in September, and Clearwater in October. In addition, we plan to participate in the Georgia Open Cup, the Capital Cup in Washington, D.C., and the Tampa Sun Bowl over Christmas.

I am very much looking forward to attending your camp July 31 through August 4. I am still very interested in playing soccer at Super College and hope to be in contact with you at camp. Enclosed is an updated list of coaches who can accurately evaluate my level of play.

Sincerely,

John Jones

Your Ticket to Success: Your Resumé

What to include with your letter changes slightly, depending on what stage you are at in school. If you have some particularly impressive statistics, including those may be worthwhile. If it's still early in your athletic career, you may want to just write a letter of introduction to show your interest and give a few specifics about your skills. If you're a sophomore or older, a resumé is probably a necessity for most schools. The resumé should include all your relevant personal information (name, address, birthday, height, weight, position), as well as your academic credentials (GPA, standardized test scores, school-related extracurriculars) and athletic background. Be specific when listing where you've played; don't just write "Varsity basketball." Instead, put down "Starter, varsity basketball (League I-A), 2001–2002."

You also want to list what club or travel teams you've played for and what major tournaments you've participated in. If you've gone to a specialty camp or traveled abroad to play, put that down, too. In essence, you want the coach to know exactly what road you took to get to the point you are currently, because that will help him to fully evaluate your talent.

Athletic Resumé

John Jones
Goalkeeper
Class of 2000

Personal Address:	1234 Street
	Somewhere, GA
	555-123-4567
	JohnJones@ZZZ.com
Parents:	Mary Louise and Paul Jones
Height:	6'
Weight:	165 pounds
Date of Birth:	9-6-81
Academics (Senior) High School:	Beacon High School Somewhere, GA
GPA:	3.43
SAT:	1090
Activities:	Fellowship of Christian Athletes (Treasurer—Sophomore, President—Junior) Student Council (Treasurer—Freshman) Young Life

---

	Varsity Basketball—Freshman, Sophomore, Junior Selected as Senior Mentor
Awards:	Commendation Award—Sophomore Honor Roll—Sophomore, Junior *Who's Who Among American High School Students*, 1998, 1999 All Northeast GA Basketball Team Honorable Mention—Junior
Soccer (High School A/AA):	Started Varsity—Freshman, Sophomore, Junior (Captain) GAA Freshman—1.37 Sophomore—1.4 Junior—1.2 Region Champs 1998 State Runner-Up 1999 All Northeast GA Soccer Team—Sophomore, Junior Voted Team MVP—Junior
Clubs:	Cavaliers YMCA 1992–1998 Knights Under-18 Sporting FC 1999 MVP of Charleston Thanksgiving Soccer Shootout 1998 (Under 18A) ODP 1994–1998 [Olympic Development Program]
Tournaments:	Athens United Invitational 1993–1997 (Winner, 1993 and 1997) Fayetteville Lightning Classic 1998 (Winner) Cocoa Expo Cup 1995 (Finalist), 1997 (Winner) Tampa Bay Sun Bowl 1994, 1996, 1998 Atlanta Cup 1993–1998 (Semifinalist 1998) Open Cup 1994–1998 (Finalist) Riverfest—Chattanooga 1998 (Finalist) Charleston Thanksgiving Shootout 1998 (Winner)

ODP Tournaments:	Super Y League 1999 Memphis, Houston, Clearwater
Camps and International Play:	Furman—2 years Ralph Lundy—4 years Number 1 Goalkeeper Camp—1 year ODP Region Camp 1997 Great Saves—4 years International Soccer—England 1995 (Team MVP) ODP Costa Rica 1997 UNC-Charlotte—1 year Creighton—1 year

Of course, to be able to have an impressive resumé, you must have tried to do impressive things. If you're trying to convince the coach at a top-level golf school that he should be interested in you but you haven't played in any of the premiere junior golf tournaments, that coach is going to be very skeptical. "It's like trying to get a job without a resumé," said one student who took up golf later in his career and did not have the credentials that many programs considered necessary.

Make Sure You're Connected

For a small percentage of elite high school athletes—the "blue chips," as they're called—the recruiting process is more about college coaches selling their universities to the student. But for the most part, if you want to play sports in college you've got to make yourself attractive to the schools on your own. That means getting the coaches to notice you and, as important, remember you.

Some families hire "college guides" to help market their children to universities. These college guides in essence act as quasi–public relations agents for student-athletes. In most cases, that's overkill. The bottom line is that most coaches want to get to know their kids as well as possible, and if there is an outside agent getting in the way—be it a "guide" or even just an overaggressive mother or father—it's that much more difficult for the coach.

Do some research before you call or write to a coach. Find out how long the coach has been at the school—if he's new, don't be afraid to ask him what sort of philosophy he brings to the program. Find out what he expects of his players in the off-season, for example, or what kind of training schedule the team keeps. Read about the team itself, and if there are opening positions (because of seniors graduating or transfers) you think you'd be perfect for, point out where you could be useful. Coaches will appreciate that you are taking the time to find out about their programs instead of merely calling and demanding information from them.

Bottom line: If you play a specialty position—like goalkeeper in soccer or lacrosse, for example—it pays to figure out what sort of availability there is for those spots on college teams. All things being equal, you'd probably rather try and beat out another freshman or unproven upperclassmen for playing time than the senior who has logged three seasons' worth of work already. Again, don't be afraid to ask the coach what he thinks about the team for the upcoming year. A question such as "Are you anticipating some changes in your lineup next season, Coach?" is not necessarily out of bounds.

Play by the Rules

Trying to explain all the rules that exist to govern recruiting is akin to trying to teach Mandarin Chinese in a week. It can't be done. To learn about the various contact dates and signing periods for collegiate athletes, your best course of action is to ask your guidance counselor for the latest copy of the NCAA newsletter, which will highlight certain parts of the academic calendar for you.

In terms of recruiting violations, the most reliable advice is to say that if something seems improper to you, you should ask someone about it. Coaches can't give you anything for coming to their school—money, gifts, etc.—and if you take anything from them or any other representatives of a university, you are on dangerous ground. Penalties for recruiting violations can include loss of eligibility, which means you'll have to sit on the sidelines while the games go on without you.

If you happen to try out with a professional team (that is, any team on which the players are paid to play) while you're still in high school, it will not affect your collegiate eligibility. There are several stipulations that go along with this, however, and you would be advised to read the current NCAA literature, which spells out specifically the criteria for allowable interactions.

As for collegiate tryouts, they are, for the most part, not allowed. A coach may watch you compete with a high school or club team, but he is not allowed to hold a tryout specifically for his own collegiate team. The only exception to this rule is that Division-II colleges are allowed to hold tryouts during the off-season of each sport. Again, there are several rules governing this procedure, and if you are asked to participate in one of these, you would be well advised to make sure it is properly run.

D-I or Bust?

You hear it all the time. A top-notch high school athlete is asked where he's planning to go to college, and he replies "I'm looking at several D-I programs." What you don't hear, however, is whether he'll get a scholarship to a D-I school or even make the team there at all.

Division I is the pinnacle of collegiate athletics when it comes to exposure, but if you're not getting a guarantee from a D-I coach about a roster spot or playing time, it might pay to ask yourself if you'd rather ride the bench at Big State University or be a starter at a smaller D-II or D-III school.

If you're reasonably sure that professional sports isn't going to be a part of your future, you're not giving up too much by opting for a smaller program. Indeed, you might actually be gaining a lot by considering the lower-division programs. The athletes at many of the lower-division schools are given more freedom to enjoy the typical college-student experience—Greek life and social clubs, for example—which can frequently be lost in the big-time D-I schools.

And don't be quick to assume that just because a D-III school doesn't have scholarships, you'll be in debt until you're 50, paying off your loans. Most D-III coaches are sensitive to the financial needs of the kids they're recruiting and will do anything they can to help you put together a proposal for aid (which can include grants as well as sports-related work-study opportunities) for the financial aid office.

Narrowing Your Choices

So you've been in contact with the coach at your dream school since you were 14, but you've also been responsible and established correspondence with coaches at smaller colleges as well, and you now have a mix of possibilities in both Division-I and Division-III schools. Good job—but now it's time to start thinking about the realities of what life as a college athlete will entail.

No doubt when you spoke with all the coaches, regardless of the level of their school, they told you that being an athlete is a commitment of time and ... well, time. There are all kinds of distractions at college, many of which can be rather attractive—flirting, parties, clubs, and just fooling around with your new friends. But being a varsity athlete severely diminishes your availability for many of those activities.

Exactly how much of your time is spent on athletics each week varies greatly from sport to sport, but you should certainly be counting on having all your classes as early in the day as possible (that's right, plenty of 8:30 classes), because most teams have practice in the afternoon. Depending on the sport, the travel load may require you to be disciplined enough to tune out the music on a long van ride so you can struggle through Aristotle or study for your anthropology test on a late-night flight.

The key, as you probably began to learn during your recruitment process, is time management. It might not seem so difficult to balance homework and practice when you're in high school, but it's a lot different when you come home after a long workout, you still have to write that six-page paper on the brain, and Mom isn't there with a warm meal on the table. Instead, you're looking at a refrigerator with three-week old sushi and your roommate's bio experiment.

Bottom line: Lest it seem like being a college athlete is akin to being some sort of POW, it's also good to know that there will be plenty of other kids pondering the nutritional value of a bio experiment, and you will likely forge terrific bonds with them. Athletes often talk about the idea of the team being an extended family, and nowhere is this more true than on the college level. Regardless of what division, the members of a college sports team share experiences that are particularly unique and that draw them together.

Making Choices

As if you hadn't had enough choices to make up to this point, you should recognize that there will be a series of trade-offs that go along with being a varsity athlete. At many schools, certain things will be forbidden—by coaches, typically—and it may seem like there are certain parts of your collegiate experience that just aren't being experienced.

There's a very good chance that, if you live in a freshman dorm, while many of your dormmates are going through fraternity or sorority rush, you may be forced to sit idly by. Oftentimes, there are customs or traditions within particular teams that are enforced like rules—team dinners or meetings or a traditional house where sophomores live, for example—and they may or may not be what you had anticipated doing on your own.

Of course, traditions and customs are one thing, but hazing is quite another. Although it's very difficult to ascertain whether or not hazing exists at a particular school (and in a particular sport), it's worthwhile to put your thinking cap on if something about some of the players seems a little off. And of course, the smart people who will be reading this book are certainly the kind of people who realize that hazing is flat-out wrong and should always be reported to the proper authorities.

Bottom line: It is never okay to be hazed. Ever.

Get to Know the School: Getting Specific

Because this is a book and not a college recruiting brochure, there will be no individual promotions for particular universities in this section. There will be a couple of ideas that you should consider as you move toward a decision about what school to attend. The first thing you should consider seems relatively elementary: You will have to go to the school you choose.

Seems silly, right? But now let's play pretend for just a second. You've arrived on campus, moved in your boxes, and set up your room—you're killing some time, so you think you'll go lift some weights at the gym. You're taking a quick jog around the track to warm up, when all of a sudden you hit an uneven patch in the ground, lurch forward, and feel an unbelievable pain shooting up through your knee. Next thing you know, you're in the hospital with a torn ACL (anterior cruciate ligament, a devastating knee injury) and the doctor is telling you that you're out of the sports scene for at least six months.

This sounds terrible, but it happens all the time. And after the shock wears off, you're stuck with a bunch of free time you didn't plan for at a school that you might not have taken the time to get to know outside of the athletic facility.

Bottom line: Make sure you know all about the school that you decide to attend—even the parts you think you might never have to use. If you happen to pick a school that has a separate dining room for athletes, check into the plans for regular students, too—you don't know when you'll have to utilize it. Check into the dorm situation if it's different for athletes, and make you'll be comfortable with the location of the school—rural, urban, or otherwise—if your time isn't perpetually occupied by athletics.

It should go without saying that you know all about the school's academic programs, but it's worth repeating: Know your options. Just because you show up your freshman year as a prebusiness football player doesn't mean that by spring break you won't be looking into student government while taking classes as a prelaw major. It pays to find out what the strengths of your chosen school are, even if they're not areas that you think you will pursue.

Finally, make sure that you get a feel for the people—I'm talking about nonathletes here—who will be walking with you on the quad and (hopefully) cheering for you on the sidelines. If you become a big star at school, you're going to want to *like* the people who are screaming your name in the bleachers, and if for whatever reason you end up in the bleachers yourself, it's a whole lot more fun to be there with some friends.

Bottom line: Although sports may seem to be the most important aspect in choosing what school you attend, there's a good chance that it may not be the most important aspect of your life while you're there. And if it isn't, you want to do everything you can beforehand to make sure that the experience is still a fantastic one.

Redshirts—More Than the Color of Your Uniform

Even if you avoid any sort of injury, there is always the possibility that you may be redshirted at some point during your athletic career. If you are redshirted, you are ineligible to participate in games for your team for an entire season. You still go to school, but you do not lose a year of athletic eligibility.

This presents you with a situation where you will have to spend more than four years at college (because every athlete has four years of eligibility). It's a situation that you should discuss with your coach to find out if it is possible (some coaches do not redshirt their players, they either cut an athlete or use him) and then consider the consequences. Is spending an extra year in college to play all four years something you think you're willing to do? This is something you want to know about as soon as possible during your decision process.

Fans of major college sports hear about redshirts most often in football and basketball, when a hot young freshman quarterback comes to a big school, for example, where a senior is already established in that position. The freshman is redshirted, and he keeps his four years of eligibility instead of using one as a backup or bench player. Hypothetically, the next year the redshirt will come in and have a spot on the team, but as you'll quickly learn if you go to a big-time school, there are few promises to be made. Do yourself a favor and be sure about whatever scenario a coach presents you, particularly if it involves redshirting. Ask about what your role will be in the following year and if you will be guaranteed a spot on the team. Also be sure that you understand how the redshirting will affect your scholarship (if you have one) and whether you will receive the same financial package in the following years.

The Latecomer

Imagine that you're a freshman at State College (not necessarily a student-athlete), and you're vacuuming the rug in your freshman-year dorm room. You're pushing the vacuum back and forth when suddenly you realize that *it's the most natural motion you've ever done in your entire life.*

So this gets you to thinking: "Hmm, maybe this rhythmic pendulum motion would translate into a perfect golf swing. Maybe I could be on the college golf team!"

Although this is not the typical story for how a walk-on makes himself known to a college coach, the concept is the same. Regardless of the reasons, if you get to school and decide that you would like to play a varsity sport, you may still be able to join the team. Go see the coach and tell him that you are interested in trying out. If you have a resumé (and some good experience), bring that along, but otherwise you should be prepared for some level of skepticism. Don't be deterred, but be willing to prove that you're skilled enough to be on the team.

Obviously, the better the school's program in your sport, the harder it will be for you to crack the roster without being recruited. But at some schools, particularly many Division-III programs, the amount of actual live recruiting is limited. Especially in some of the minor sports such as track and swimming, tryouts are the norm, and preseason practices (occasionally run by captains or upperclassmen) are the best way to gauge where your skill level falls in relation to others.

Many schools will include a survey or questionnaire in the packet you receive along with your acceptance letter. In many cases, your answers to the questions relating to sports will determine whether your name is passed along to the relevant varsity coach, who may then get in touch with you over the summer. If this happens, take it at face value; you are not committing to anything, and it's likely that the coach isn't either. He probably just wants to get a feel for the types of people who may or may not be trying out for his team in the fall and is looking to add some background to skeleton information he received from the admissions office.

Once you arrive on campus, make the coach's office one of your first stops. This will allow him to put a face to the name he's got, and you'll have made an impression as someone who will be a dedicated member of the team, if given the chance. Tell the coach what you've been doing, training-wise, over the summer, and ask him if there are any informal workouts before school starts or during orientation. If he's not entirely receptive, ask if he would mind giving you the phone numbers of some of the older members of the team or the captains, and give them a call. Let them know that you just got to school and are wondering what they're doing to get in shape for the upcoming season—more often than not, they'll be more than happy to share the information, and possibly a workout, with you.

Some coaches choose not to schedule tryouts during the regular season. As Ralph Polson, associate head soccer coach at College of Charleston, South Carolina, explains, "Due to the limitations on the number of practices during preseason, we limit our walk-on tryouts in the fall. Because we also participate in spring training, we hold a walk-on tryout in January for student-athletes who weren't recruited but are interested in joining the team." The odds of success, he notes, are small but worth the effort if your dream is to play and you have the skills they need.

The Local Scene

If you're one of the better players on your high school team, it's likely that at one point or another, a local college coach may approach you after a game to talk about "staying at home for school."

If this happens, it's worth asking about what brought the coach to this particular game or tournament. Frequently, a coach will come to look at one player, realize that it's unlikely that he will be able to attract the player to his school, then make contact with someone else. There's nothing wrong with this, but obviously it will matter to you if the coach came to see you in the first place.

Because the cost of attending many schools is significantly less for in-state residents, the flexibility that a local coach has with money can be far greater than that of a coach who is working with national players who are responsible for paying full tuitions. If you're someone who anticipates needing a large amount of financial aid, you're probably already considering in-state schools anyway. But if you aren't, it's an avenue that's well worth exploring.

"They could have given me two scholarships, and I still wouldn't have gone there because it wasn't the kind of experience I wanted," said one New Jersey resident about a local college. This student was smart, because he knew what sort of college he wanted to go to and didn't settle for something less than what he wanted just because he had an opportunity to play sports. "After all, wherever I went, sports weren't going to be my life," he added.

Bottom line: Local schools are definitely worth a look—a serious one, in many cases. But like everything else in your college search, you have to look at the whole picture and recognize the pros and cons of every situation.

Playing for Fun

What do sports say about a person? Plenty of things (good and bad), depending on who you ask. If you're asking an admissions counselor, it's a good bet that playing sports in high school will only help your application. Not only does it show a well-rounded side to you, but it also indicates that you're able to effectively manage your time and keep track of your priorities, as well as function in a team-oriented setting.

If you think your playing days will be over once you hit the road for college, you're probably mistaken. Even if you have no aspirations of playing on the varsity level, intramural sports are available at nearly every college in the country. In fact, at many schools the intensity over intramurals outweighs the passion for the school's varsity teams!

At most schools, two or three major sports are run during each semester (for example, football, basketball, and soccer in the fall; softball, court hockey, and volleyball in the spring) as well as a sprinkling of smaller seasons and one-day events in sports as random as badminton and kickball. Play is usually offered on several different levels, often featuring fraternities and sororities in one league and unaffiliated teams in another. However the leagues are divided, it's usually easy enough to figure out what skill level you want to compete at, so even the biggest "glory days" jock can get his sports fix.

Add to Your College Box

You want to maintain a complete file on your high school athletic career.

- Each year, keep a list of your teams and what positions you played. Include not only those teams at school, but also any recreational, community, house of worship, club, and travel teams.

- Include any newspaper write-ups of your games and especially those articles that mention you.

- Add any awards or honors you've received for your athletics, including any that might be Scholar-Athlete awards (these honor students who combine outstanding athletic ability and good grades).

- Keep a list of all athletic workshops and camps you attend.

If you hope to be a college-recruited athlete, start a separate College Box dedicated to your athletic career and recruitment information.

- Include a copy of the NCAA rules for recruiting.
- Keep a careful log of any contacts with coaches.
- Add in copies of all letters or e-mails you send to or receive from coaches, and make notes following any telephone contacts.
- Keep a copy of any videotape that you send to coaches.

What You Need to Know

- Middle school sports teams are the farm system for high school athletics. If you want to play on the varsity team, suit up in middle school.
- You will need to play on an elite level, outside of school, if you hope to be recruited by a college coach. This takes an enormous investment of time and money.
- Never choose a college strictly on the basis of athletics. You need to consider how you would like the school if you were injured and unable to play. Would you still choose that college?

Chapter 3

The Inside Scoop on Extracurricular Activities

Coming Up in This Chapter

- What your extracurricular activities tell colleges about you
- How to find the right club for you
- Start something new
- The role of community service

Joining clubs is easy; making a valuable contribution to each one is the hard part. Don't join any club unless you're interested in the activity—your time is too valuable. Don't sign up for loads of clubs just to pad your resumé, either. College admissions officers can easily see through that ruse. They want to know that you do more with your time than just study, and your extracurricular activities tell them a lot about you.

Extracurricular activities are any things you do with your time beyond your studies. They can be programs sponsored by the school or those under the aegis of your community, house of worship, or any outside organization. You may also spend your free time doing some form of service, for example, volunteering in a soup kitchen, tutoring, working on environmental-related issues, or joining a political campaign.

You Are More Than Just Grades

Even when you were just a little kid in preschool, you were learning—becoming educated—through play. One study has shown that there is a direct correlation between the amount of hours children spend playing with blocks in nursery school and the likelihood of their taking an advanced physics class in high school! Preschool educators understand that kids learn through doing. That's true for teens, too.

You'll learn as much from the extracurricular activities you choose to join as you will from the classes you take. And colleges will learn more about you as an individual by looking at the clubs and groups you join than they will by checking your grades and SAT scores.

Here's why. College is more than a collection of great professors and interesting courses. If you are only looking for class work, you might consider instead an online or long-distance-learning program. And even then you'd be missing something, because you learn as much from your fellow classmates as you do from your professors and textbooks.

So when college admissions officers are building a class (and that's the way they refer to the admissions process), they're looking for more than a 4.0 GPA and an SAT score of 1600. Frankly, for the most selective schools, an entire class could easily be filled with valedictorians boasting high standardized test scores. And they could bore themselves to death, too!

But that's not what they're looking for. They're looking for students who will enrich the college life. Sure, they want smart kids to enhance the intellectual community, but equally important are students who will add to the college socially, athletically, musically, artistically, dramatically, etc. They are looking for students who volunteer in ways that make the world a better place, environmentally, politically, and ethically.

Colleges look for active students and know they have to provide an outlet for their interests once they enroll. You'll see it in the recruiting material you will receive. For example, Bowdoin College, a liberal arts college in Maine, makes clear on their website, "If you have been very active in your school or community, you will love what you find at Bowdoin.

With two theaters, 29 varsity athletic teams, all kinds of community service activities, more than 100 student-led organizations, our own radio and cable TV operations, as well as more than 1,000 scheduled on-campus events annually, there are an enormous number of opportunities for you to play an active role." And this is at school with only 1,621 students!

Bottom line: Starting in middle school and continuing throughout high school, you will want to not only join clubs, but to make a meaningful contribution to them as well.

When It's All About Numbers

There are some public universities where, if you are an in-state student, your admission is determined by meeting certain grade and/or standardized test criteria. For example, at the University of Iowa, if you live in state and are within the top 30 percent of your class, you are assured of admission. If this applies to you, do you still have to worry about extracurricular activities?

Yes, says Michael Barron, director of admissions for the University of Iowa. The additional information gained from a student's extracurricular activities is exactly what makes the difference for those who aren't admitted strictly by the numbers. There is a section of the application where you can indicate if you want "special consideration." This special consideration allows you to argue your case about why you should be admitted to the university if you don't meet the class/rank formula. You can explain how your interests and extracurricular activities will help make you a productive member of the university community.

All colleges are willing to listen to your explanation of why you should be admitted even if you don't meet their usual standards. If there is no obvious place to state your case on the application, write a separate letter and attach it to your forms.

Middle School Clubs

Don't ignore the clubs and activities sponsored by your middle school. Like sports teams (see Chapter 2), junior high school clubs can serve as training grounds for the clubs and organizations you will find in high school. Your work in the school orchestra, for the debate team, or in the video club, for example, will serve you well when you hit high school. Although your junior high participation will not appear on your college application as your high school participation will, it will give you an edge so you can take a leadership position in high school programs earlier than if you didn't have this experience.

Make New Friends and Keep the Old Ones

Don't join a club just to be with your friends if you don't enjoy the activity. Equally important, don't avoid a program if none of your friends will join with you. In fact, expanding your circle of friends to include new ones you'll meet in new clubs is one of the most important benefits of joining extracurricular activities. You'll need that kind of courage when you head off to college and are confronted with an entire university full of people you don't know. Plus, while in high school, with its ups and downs of friendships, you'll appreciate these new pals and their support when things aren't perfect with your usual group of buddies.

Are All Clubs Equal?

As far as college admissions go, should you join the service club, become a cheerleader, play a sport, or work on the newspaper? It doesn't matter. The choice of which activity is right for you should be made based on what you enjoy doing and, for your own self-esteem, one in which you can get more proficient. Don't stick with the orchestra if you've come to hate practicing your instrument. Move on and find something you enjoy and want to spend the time getting better at.

Bottom line: Colleges don't care what you do, but they do want you to do something. Colleges want to see that you have pursued an interest, learned from it, and grown because of it.

Quality vs. Quantity

So how many extracurricular activities do you need to look good on your college application?

Forget numbers. This is truly a case of less is more. Better you should have been actively involved in one or two groups—spending 10 hours a week on them—than to have a laundry list of clubs on your application.

You can't fool college admissions officers. They can spot a phony club—one that has been created for the express purpose of padding your application, such as the underwater basket-weaving club—at 10 paces.

Furthermore, colleges require you to list how long you've been a member of any organization you list on your application. So it's fine if you join an activity in your senior year if it's because you like what the club does. But don't expect to get a lot of credit for your participation in a group for less than two years. You might get credit if your short tenure in the club is because the program is new and couldn't have existed before, for example, if you headed up an ad hoc group to raise funds for a community devastated by a natural disaster. You may also get credit if you can convincingly explain why you didn't discover this interest until late in your high school career, for example, you received a bike for your seventeenth birthday and joined the school's cycling team shortly afterward.

What shows your real commitment to an activity? Take the example of how one student explored his interest in sports, specifically soccer:

- He was the goalie on his high school's junior varsity and then varsity teams.
- He played on an elite traveling soccer team since fourth grade.
- He attended goalie camps for several summers throughout high school.
- One summer he was selected for a soccer team that played in tournaments in England and Sweden.
- He got his soccer referee's certification at 16 and earned spending money as a soccer ref throughout high school.
- He served as the sports editor of the high school newspaper.

The point is that this student explored his interest from several different angles, not just playing soccer.

Finding Something You Like to Do

What do you enjoy doing in your spare time? Reading? Playing sports? Cooking? Working on computers? Dancing? Writing? Traveling? Whatever you like doing, develop ways of using your interests to enrich yourself as an individual—which is exactly what colleges are hoping you will do.

Make a list of the things you enjoy doing in your free time. Include those things you are passionate about, then add those activities you don't know much about but wish you did. Maybe your list includes music, skate-boarding, and the environment. It doesn't matter what's on your list. Don't try to find something that looks good on paper or to match your interests to the clubs that currently exist. Be honest and include those things that make you happy or just spark your interest.

Then make a list of the clubs that currently exist in your middle school and high school. Maybe it's an obvious match. You like to write poetry, and your high school has a literary magazine. That was easy.

Now go outside of school. Include programs and opportunities for service in your house of worship, in national organizations such as 4-H, or in your community.

There are many ways to contribute to an organization. You can even do it at a distance if there's not a chapter in or near your town. Find an organization in which you believe, for example, the Red Cross, Green-peace, or the Sierra Club, and either start a local chapter or fund-raise for the group in your community. Love to sing? Organize an evening of entertainment as a fund-raiser for your favorite charity. There are many great ways to combine interests if you think about it.

Scout Success

If you're in middle school and still active in the Boy Scouts or Girl Scouts, this is no time to stop. First and most important of all, you should remain a Scout if you enjoy the activities. As an older Scout, you will have many more leadership opportunities and much more freedom in the types of projects you can pursue. And colleges are very impressed by any teen that remains a Scout. Why? To earn Boy Scout Eagle Scout rank or the Girl Scout Gold Award represents years of commitment and hard work.

For example, according to the Boy Scouts of America website, to earn the Eagle Scout rank—the highest advancement rank in Scouting—you have to "fulfill requirements in the areas of leadership, service, and outdoor skills." Only about 4 percent of all Boy Scouts earn this rank. You must earn 21 merit badges including those in First Aid, Citizenship in the Community, Citizenship in the Nation, Personal Fitness, Personal Management, Camping, and Family Life. The remaining badges take considerable time and effort to earn.

The Girl Scout Gold Award is the highest award a Senior Scout can earn. As the Girl Scouts of America website points out, "It symbolizes outstanding accomplishments in the areas of leadership, community service, career planning and personal development." Fewer than 3 percent of Senior Girl Scouts win this award. The Scout must develop her own plan for winning this award. Her Girl Scout council then approves her plan. It takes one to two years to complete the requirements of this award.

Bottom line: Colleges are impressed by high schoolers who are still Boy or Girl Scouts. These kids make the kind of commitment to an activity that schools appreciate. They give back to the community in which they live.

Finding Time

A good executive understands that maintaining an up-to-date calendar is the key to seamless scheduling. Finding enough time to balance all your responsibilities, including those that your extracurricular activities demand, is a lesson in itself. That's why you need to look at the school year as a whole as well as in blocks of time. To help keep track of your time and the activities you're responsible for, try the following:

- Buy a large calendar and write down what activities meet on which days. Be sure to include games, performances, and extra holiday events. Note religious obligations (holidays, services, and instruction), birthdays, and family events. Now not only can you tell where you need to be and when at a glance, but this also forces you to focus on how much time you will actually have to do all that needs to be done.

- Keep the calendar up to date and mark down every exam scheduled, when reports or projects are due, and any other academic requirements, including any standardized testing, as the year progresses.

By keeping a calendar, you can determine when you have blocks of time available and when you will be pressed and stressed—and then make the necessary adjustments. For example, if you play a varsity sport in the fall, you don't want to take on much more in your other activities because the sport is a huge time commitment by itself. Or if you are in the school orchestra, which meets twice a week before school, you may feel comfortable joining a club that meets only one afternoon a month. Or if you volunteer somewhere in your community or take religious instruction one night a week or have music lessons on a weekly basis, you will need to reduce your other outside activities.

Bottom line: If you hold a part-time job, that needs to be part of your time management equation as well. Although working is impressive to colleges and you may need the money, your first priority must be school. You may need to limit your extracurricular activities to accommodate your work demands and school demands. Try to find time for at least one outside school or community service activity.

If the Club Doesn't Exist

If your school or community doesn't sponsor an organization that follows your interests, then it's time for you to do something about it. *Start your own.* That kind of leadership and initiative is good for you in general terms and also shows colleges the stuff you're made of.

Perhaps you see the need for a more specialized group. For example, if your school has a band, but you enjoy playing jazz, you may want to see if the school would be interested in sponsoring a smaller jazz ensemble group. If not, you may still want to put together one on your own and perform locally for interested groups. One high school sophomore organized a singing group of three girls and three boys. By word of mouth, they began playing for small fund-raisers and at local senior centers.

It's important to remember though, that, as the chief organizer of the choral group points out, "I wasn't concerned about how [organizing a singing group] looked on my college applications. I would have done it anyway, because I love to sing." It was, in fact, an impressive addition to her portfolio.

If you want to start your own program, here are some tips:

1. Determine if there is a group of people you know who are interested in a particular activity. You might already be meeting informally. If not, arrange a meeting and post the date, time, and place on student bulletin boards, asking for other interested students to join you.

2. Find a faculty member who will be willing to supervise the club. This is necessary for any club that will meet on school grounds.

3. Write up a proposal, indicating the kind of club you hope to start, the number of students likely to be interested, the faculty advisor, and any funding you think will be necessary. Indicate where you think the funding might come from. The board of education? PTA funds? The principal? Student fund-raising?

4. Present the proposal to the principal or student activities director. In order to meet on school grounds, you will need administrative approval.

Case study: Two middle school students (eighth graders) wanted to start a school newspaper. They spent time over the summer before school started enlisting other students to sign up for the newspaper staff (making sure that sixth and seventh graders also joined). Next, they wrote up a proposal, and at the start of the school year, they presented it to the principal. Although he approved their proposal, he could not secure funding for the paper and, therefore, couldn't hire a faculty advisor for the group. The two students then found a parent volunteer to supervise the program, and the principal agreed to fund the project's printing costs from his discretionary funds (although he might have approached the PTA). Finally, the students approached the high school newspaper staff to help start the program and learn about layout, design, and organization. This was important because it opened a path between middle school student activities and high school clubs. This also meant that the following year, when the eighth graders entered high school, they could join the newspaper staff already experienced and able to take more responsibility than average freshman. It was a win-win situation.

An interesting twist on this story: In the years that followed, the high school newspaper instituted a formal volunteer program to serve as mentors to the middle school newspaper. This helped the younger students as well as enriched the college applications of the high schoolers.

If you're not planning on meeting on school grounds, but, say, meet at a local park or rotate to group members' homes for meetings, you don't need a faculty member sponsor, the proposal, the administrative approval, etc. Certainly a school-sponsored group you created will look impressive on your resumé and transcripts, but a nonschool-sponsored group will look good, too. You're still showing the initiative and leadership that college admissions officers are looking for.

Leadership Counts

You don't have to be president of every club you join, but being an officer or assuming additional responsibilities does reflect a growing commitment to the group on your part. That's important for your own personal growth—and what colleges are interested in seeing. They need leaders on campus—people who are willing to make things happen. Displaying leadership qualities shows that you are self-motivated and responsible. These are the keys to handling the academic and social demands of college.

Being a leader in a group is also an example of good time management—assuming, of course, that you are handling your schoolwork and extracurricular activities well. (See the following "Time Management Tips" section for signs of stress.)

You don't have to be the top dog in every club or activity you're involved in. Here are some ideas to help fight that "I *have* to be president or I won't get into college" feeling:

- **Pick your battles.** Sure, the title or lead role looks good, but there's no sense in becoming an officer or leading member of the cast unless you believe in the organization and are willing to commit time and effort to its goals. Don't try to be the president or leader of every club or activity you're involved with. Narrow your efforts to just the few that are most important to you. It's better to do one or two jobs well, because you still have to keep up your studies.

  It's fine to be a member of some organizations, without assuming a leadership position, if you just enjoy the company and the activity. You might love the roar of the greasepaint and smell of the crowd, but you can't handle getting home at 8 P.M. from rehearsal five days a week and still face four hours of homework. If you want to take a leading role in a play, make sure that you cut back on other extracurricular activities.

- **Plan ahead.** Freshman year is a time to try different activities without necessarily making a long-term commitment to any one of them. But as you begin to narrow your focus to just a few clubs, think about the contributions you'd like to make to each by the time you graduate. One student knew from the first day she entered high school that she wanted to be in a leadership position in the music honor society. Music was her passion, and she wanted to devote most of her efforts to the various groups in her high school (as well as her church). Other students might decide they want to make a varsity team and perhaps even serve as team captain. Whatever your choice, only assume a leadership position if you believe in the organization and want to make a real contribution to its efforts.

- **Winning by default.** Sometimes you become president by default when nobody else will take the job. Accept the position only if you have the time and interest, not to pad your application. If you're going to do a job, do it well.

- **Negotiate titles.** Let's be honest. Titles look good on college applications, and the competition can become intense for the top spots in an organization. For example, you want to be editor-in-chief of the school newspaper but so do three other well-qualified students. The solution? Make it a win-win situation for everyone. Think job-sharing and creative titles. You'll feel better (and so will the others) if you have more free time, feel respected, and get a good title for your college applications. Plus, you'll be able to accomplish much more in the organization if there are more people willing to assume responsibility.

Job-sharing is common in the real world; why shouldn't it also exist in high school extracurricular activities? Divide up the responsibilities of the job or offer to alternate. On one high school newspaper, by sharing the top leadership position, one editor was able to take the lead in the fall play because she knew her counterpart would shoulder more of the daily responsibilities during the rehearsal period and run of the play. On the other hand, the other editor-in-chief was able to continue his participation in the winter season of his varsity sport because he, too, knew that the newspaper wouldn't suffer during his absence.

Develop a list of acceptable leadership titles. For a newspaper, these might be deputy editor, managing editor, editorial page editor, executive editor, etc. Don't be limited by the titles that have previously existed—there's no reason why you can't develop new titles to meet the needs and acknowledge the efforts of the members of the group. Businesses do it all the time when they want to retain a valued member of the team. Don't worry that colleges will think less of you if you don't have the top spot. Every day they reject tons of club presidents who don't have much else going for them. Your goal should be to show a progression over the years in the amount of responsibility you have been willing to assume.

- **Toot your own horn.** When completing your application, outline special accomplishments you've achieved during your time in a club. If you organized the largest fund-raising event in school history, increased membership by 25 percent, or the newspaper won an award on your watch, be sure to add that to your application. If necessary, add a supplementary paper to your application, detailing your accomplishments. You need to make sure that the admissions officer understands your successes.

Bottom line: Schools want to see that you have a passion for something and that you take that interest and pursue it, learn from it, and share it with others. Over the four years of high school, make a stronger commitment to a club and assume a leadership position.

Community Service

What's the best reason to do volunteer work? Because it's the right thing to do and you'll feel better about yourself for having done it. To quote President John F. Kennedy, "Ask not what your country can do for you; ask what you can do for your country." That's it in a nutshell.

Each of us is expected to give back, volunteer, or somehow contribute to the world we live in. There's no one way or best way to volunteer. If you love animals, walk into the animal shelter and volunteer for a few hours a week. They need people to clean cages, walk the dogs, play with the cats, etc. As one full-time staffer at an animal shelter pointed out, "I started here as a volunteer when I was 16. It's a great way to find out if you want to work in the field."

Like young children? Check out the day-care centers in your community. They always need extra hands to read one-on-one with little kids, offer homework help, or just color and keep some youngsters company.

Senior citizen homes also can use volunteers to spend time with the residents, serve food trays, assist with arts and crafts programs, transport residents from one part of the home to another, etc.

Interested in the environment? Join a local group dedicated to improving your own community by cleaning up beaches, parks, old cemeteries, local monuments, etc.

To volunteer in some facilities …

- You may need to get a work permit. Generally you can get your working papers from your school guidance office. To apply, you will need parental permission and proof of age.

- You may be asked to make a certain time commitment. Organizations need this for scheduling purposes as well as consistency in routine. It's time-consuming to break in new volunteers. Be realistic about what you can offer, perhaps increasing your hours during school vacations and summer breaks.

- Especially in nursing home and child-care centers, you may need to show proof of good health, that you have been vaccinated against certain diseases, and that you have had a tuberculosis (TB) test within the year.

- You may need to undergo a training period so that you can be an effective volunteer.

Bottom line: Volunteer work enriches your life even more than the lives you touch. This isn't about college at all—but of course, it does show colleges the kind of person you really are.

Volunteer Work Can Lead to $$

Another bonus of working as a volunteer is that you are first in line when a paid position opens. You may have an easier time finding a summer job if you apply to an organization where you have already been working as a volunteer.

Letters of Recommendation

If you have been actively involved in an extracurricular activity or community service project, you might want to ask the supervising adult to write a letter of recommendation for you to be sent to the colleges to which you are applying. As discussed in Chapter 7, you don't want to overdo these types of letters, but one that can give additional insight into your interests and passions can be very helpful.

One girl had been active in a Shakespearean acting group for four years. The group was loosely affiliated with the high school, and the director was a middle school teacher. The work was hard and time-consuming—and the director wrote a detailed, glowing letter of recommendation with the girl's early decision application (see Chapter 8 for more on early decision applications). The letter could explain the time, effort, and extent of the student's commitment to this outside activity, as well as her growth over four years.

Another student began volunteering at the local historical society in ninth grade. In his junior year, the organization offered him a paid internship for the summer. A letter of recommendation from the president of the organization, detailing the boy's interest in history and independent projects he had completed for the society, accompanied the student's college applications. This reinforced the essays the student had written for the application as well as bolstered his statement that he intended to major in history.

You're the Volunteer, but Who's the Driver?

Discuss your volunteer work with your parents if it will involve their time, too, for example, in the form of driving you to and from work, helping you with projects, etc. Before you make a commitment, be sure you know how you will get to the site, any expenses involved, and whether the program is adequately supervised.

Religious Activities

Be sure to include on your college application any youth group and leadership positions you hold in programs sponsored by your house of worship. Your religious commitment is another side of you that will help a college understand who you are. If you have given the youth sermon, acted as the youth liaison to the board of trustees of your house of worship, participated in religious services in a leadership role (such as reading from the Torah or serving as an altar boy), were active in the youth group and perhaps on the regional level, include these activities in the details of how you spend your time.

Time Management Tips

You are taking the most challenging course schedule possible; you're studying for the SATs; you've got chores to do at home, family responsibilities, and friends who are asking you to hang out. And although you totally enjoy the two clubs you've joined, they are taking up way too much of your time. Frankly, you're at the point where you're running out of time, energy, and enthusiasm. Sounds like burnout. Here are the signs that you need to take action to get life back in balance:

1. **Are you having trouble staying awake in class?** All students sometimes want to doze off (so do teachers), but if this is a regular occurrence, it may be a sign that you are overdoing things.

2. **Are your grades beginning to slip?** It could just be an isolated case, but if you are starting to struggle with your schoolwork, you may need to rethink your priorities. If you're worried that if you drop your outside activity, it will count against you when you apply to college, remember that the number-one item on the application is your transcript. Grades come first. Plus, you can always pick up some extracurricular activities during the summer to round out your portfolio.

3. **Are you feeling stressed out?** Are you crying a lot? Are you yelling at everyone? Or are you feeling like you can't handle your life? Stop and figure out if it's just temporary extra stress (will life get better once midterms are over?) or drop some of the extras in your life and concentrate on what you can handle.

Bottom line: Learn to say no.

One of the most important words that an executive learns is "No." You might add "No, thank you," but you do have to realize that you can't be all things to all people. You might be one of those students who everybody knows can handle most challenges, that you'll come in and save the day, if necessary. But keep in mind that you can't be effective if you are stretched too thin.

Add to Your College Box

In your College Box (see Chapter 1), keep a running list of all your extracurricular activities and service projects. Maintain the list throughout the year, because it's easy to forget the details as time passes. Include the following:

- The name of the school club or organization (if outside the school)
- Its purpose
- Your title
- What you actually did
- The name of the supervising adult
- Any awards, certificates, or honors you received

This will simplify your college application process, because you will have all the information you need to complete the section on extracurriculars and community service.

What You Need to Know

- Find activities that excite you, and invest time in them.
- Depth is better than breadth when choosing extracurricular activities. It's better to commit yourself to two or three organizations than to dabble in dozens.
- Schedule time for service projects. It makes you a better person and enriches your college applications.
- If the stress of extracurricular activities is getting to you, it's time to reevaluate how you spend your time. Remember that your grades are your first priority.

Chapter 4

Summertime: The Living Is Easy, Interesting, and Fun

Coming Up in This Chapter

- Studying for fun and profit in the summer
- Working for pay
- Volunteer work can be valuable for students and the future
- Taking the grand tour—travel opportunities in the summer

You've worked hard all year. You studied, joined a sports team, wrote for the school newspaper, and volunteered in a soup kitchen. Now school is out. What's next? The Beach? Camp? Classes? Travel? A job? In this chapter I'll cover all the possibilities to make the summer fun, relaxing, and full of personal growth. And yes, colleges do ask what you did with your summers. In this chapter, I'll give you some possible answers.

Why Summer Counts

No one is suggesting that you spend the summer with your nose in a book (although to be honest, you should always be reading something, vacation or not). But while summer vacation is a wonderful opportunity to get some much needed rest and relaxation, it's also a time to explore new interests or focus more intensely on those activities you already enjoy.

College applications almost always have a section that asks how you spent your summers. No one is expecting you to win the Nobel Peace Prize between June and September, but schools will want to see that you used your time well, and that can mean a wide range of activities, including jobs, travel, study, volunteer work, camps, and more. None of the experiences have to be earth-shattering. In fact, some of the best summer experiences are low-key. But it does mean that at the end of the summer, you've learned something about yourself and maybe about the world.

Can I Still Have Fun?

Absolutely. No summer experience, by itself, is going to get you into college. Okay, maybe if you do win the Nobel Peace Prize it would make a difference, but otherwise, the reason schools want to know how you spend your summers is because it gives them another insight into who you are. It tells them a little more about what you enjoy doing, whether you like to challenge yourself, and how you like to spend your free time. Corky Surbeck, director of admissions at Goucher College, Towson, Maryland, explains, "Anything a college-bound student can do that helps them successfully transition from secondary school to freshman year at the college of their choice is a good thing. Maybe this can come in the form of gaining self-confidence as a result of summer theater. Maybe it will be sharper writing skills as a result of a summer internship. Maybe it will be a sharper overall focus as a result of a demanding 50-hour per week summer job."

Bottom line: There is no one activity that is right for everyone. You need to figure out what is right for you and how best you will learn and grow during your summer vacations.

Mix and Match

So what do you want to do in the summer? This isn't a trick question. You should take some time to think through not only what you might enjoy doing this summer, but also in the years ahead. That way, you might agree that it would be fun to attend camp for another year, but the following summer, you might try a more academic program. Or divide your summer into multiple activities as one high school junior did: She spent the first half of her summer at a theater camp (her passion) and spent the second half working for pay in an insurance office.

Surbeck points out that "students are doing more during their summers. What I see more is students doing a little bit of a lot of activities. Most students do not have one activity that speaks for their time from the end of school to the start of school the following year. Summer opportunities are becoming like college January sessions. Get a big dose in a short period."

Take a blank piece of paper and write down all the things you want to do this summer. Your list might include the following:

- Sleep late
- Enjoy the warm weather
- Swim daily
- Challenge yourself physically
- Revel in no classes
- Hang out with friends
- Earn some money
- Travel
- Study something different
- Accelerate your coursework
- Go to camp
- Have an internship in a field you are considering as a major
- Prepare for the SAT
- Volunteer or work for some service organization
- Rest and relax after an incredibly difficult school year
- Improve your sports abilities
- Read *War and Peace* in Russian
- All of the above? None of the above?

See something that helps you narrow down your choices for the summer? For example, you might not love the warm weather, so finding a job or activity that keeps you outdoors eight hours a day isn't a priority for you. Feeling overwhelmed by the press of coursework during the school year? One solution is to take the summer off from academics. Or to help relieve the pressure of the upcoming fall term, you might take one of the tough classes over the summer, thus reducing your courseload in the fall.

You will need parental input and approval for any decision you make about your summer activities, and it will help you and your parents if you think carefully about what you would like to do. Your conversation will be easier and more focused if you can articulate your reasons for choosing one activity over another or for rejecting one of their suggestions. Here's where talking and listening with an open mind is going to be critical for both you and your parents.

Bottom line: Choosing a summer activity needs to work for everyone in the family. It will be influenced by economics as well as interests. You need to consider whether your summer ventures are going to cost money or involve your parents in the form of your transportation. Furthermore, the terrorist attacks of September 11, 2001, may well affect your parents' feelings about where you spend your summer. They may not want you too far from home.

Summer Camp—Same Old Thing or Something New?

If you've been attending sleep-away summer camp programs for several years, you might enjoy returning to familiar stomping grounds after a long school year. There is the comfort of seeing old friends and the reassurance of participating in activities you already know you enjoy. Many programs have activities for campers up to age 15, so you can attend for many years.

If you are going to return to camp, see if you can set new goals for yourself. For example, consider getting your lifeguard certification (which will be useful when you want to get a job), or assume responsibility for an arts project, theater event, or sports team. Whatever your camp has to offer, stretch yourself so that at the end of the summer you will feel like you have accomplished something new.

If you are over 15 and still love camp, consider returning as a member of the staff. You could be a counselor-in-training (CIT), sometimes called a junior counselor, a position for 15- and 16-year-olds. Other camps hire teens as part of the kitchen help. Your parents might have to pay tuition (usually at a reduced rate), but you will probably earn tips at the end of the summer.

The advantages of taking a junior staff position include the following:

- You're in a familiar environment with friends.
- You gain experience that will help when you want to get other jobs, plus have work-related references.
- If you return as a counselor in later years, you will probably receive a higher salary because you have had experience.
- Working as a CIT teaches you problem-solving skills, gives you insight into whether you might want to work with kids as a career, and lets you learn how to work as part of a team.

The last three advantages are all lessons that a college would be delighted to see that you have learned.

However, before you accept a staff position at camp, you and your parents need to be sure what exactly will be your duties and schedule. And remember, it's one thing to be at camp when you are the paying customer but another thing when you are the help. Make sure you are comfortable with the changed role.

Whatever the camp position, you will want to know the following:

- Your exact responsibilities
- Who your supervisor will be when you are working as well as when you are off
- Who your co-workers will be
- Where you will live

- ☞ What happens if you don't like your assignment
- ☞ How, if at all, you will be paid
- ☞ How much you can participate in regular camp activities, for example, can you use the facilities when you are off-duty or can you participate in team sports?

Bottom line: Going back to camp can be a fun experience, but make sure that you push yourself to try new things, even within the context of a familiar environment.

Is More School in the Picture?

You may want to consider going to summer school, either for enrichment or acceleration purposes. In some programs, you have the opportunity to study a topic in more depth. For an academic subject, such as a writing seminar, you might focus on different genres such as narrative nonfiction, short stories, or poetry. Or it could be a combination of classroom work and field studies, such as an archaeological dig or meteorological field-work.

Some students opt for something entirely outside of their usual schoolwork. For example, if you are a teenage girl interested in business, you might consider Camp $tart-Up (www.independentmeans.com), a one or two-week program developed for young women just like you. Held at various locations across the nation, students study business skills such as marketing, operations, and finance; develop a business plan; work with business technology; and even learn how to network. The course also teaches leadership skills to build self-confidence; focuses on the importance of teamwork in a business setting; and introduces negotiation techniques, business etiquette, and stress management (which can help with academic stress, too!). One girl enrolled in the program after eighth grade, came back the summer after her junior as an assistant, and ended up applying early decision (and being accepted) to Wharton, the University of Pennsylvania's top-ranked business school.

The Advantages and Disadvantages of Summer Academic Programs

There are pluses and minuses of pursuing academics during the summer. If you enjoy academics, it might not be a burden to take courses during your vacation. On the other hand, carefully consider whether it will be more or less difficult to return to school in the fall if you have spent your summer in a classroom.

The advantages of an academic summer include the following:

- The opportunity to focus on a single subject which may improve your grade in that class. For example, if you want to take AP biology but worry that it will be too stressful to take during the school year along with all your other courses, consider taking the class in a summer program. While the pace of the coursework is obviously accelerated, it will be your only academic subject and you can concentrate on it without other distractions.

- The chance to enrich your high school program. One student took an advanced math class over the summer, did well, and was admitted to her high school's honors math class in the fall.

- The option of taking classes you otherwise can't fit into your regular school program.

- The opportunity to earn enough college credits to accelerate your undergraduate degree. By taking summer programs and other AP classes during the regular school year, you could finish college in three years instead of four.

- The chance, if you attend an academic program on a college campus, to preview the school and the surrounding area.

- The pleasure, if you are a good student, of doing something in summer you enjoy doing and, in fact, do well—learning.

- If you attend the more prestigious programs, either in the United States or abroad, you have the opportunity to meet a diverse group of students and faculty—a valuable experience by itself.

But there are disadvantages of attending an academic summer program as well:

☞ While there is the intellectual challenge of new courses, you may be doing the safe thing by taking the tough course in the summer. You know how to be a good student, and you could probably handle the more challenging course during the regular school year, so maybe you should try something else to stretch yourself.

☞ You may have an unrealistic idea about a college based on spending the summer there. Often, summer programs merely rent space from the college, and the teachers are not necessarily affiliated with the university. Nor are the students on campus necessarily the students who are enrolled during the regular college term. They may simply be local students who are taking summer school classes as you are. Furthermore, you may not get an accurate perspective of the school. Summertime on a campus is generally not representative of the college during the school year. A summer on a Maine college campus can be delightful—but you have to also want to be in Maine during the winter before you apply to any college in that state!

☞ College admissions officers warn that attending their school for a summer session rarely helps ensure admission to the school.

☞ If you accelerate your program during the summer, what will you do in the fall? Be sure you have course options to take in high school, rather than place yourself out by taking too many classes during the summer. Otherwise, you may have created more problems for yourself (see Chapter 1 for finding academic programs online and in area colleges while still in high school).

How to Find the Right Program

There are enrichment programs for every possible interest, in a wide range of academic disciplines and the arts. Here's how to find them:

☞ Go local. Check your own high school as well as area colleges, adult-education programs, and private schools. You will find enrichment, acceleration, and remedial programs.

☞ Check your high school youth employment office or guidance counselor's office. In addition to job offerings, many also have information on summer academic programs.

☞ Talk to your favorite teachers. They often know about enrichment programs in their subject area. The music department teachers, for example, may be teaching at summer music camps. They can steer you to broad, general programs or more specific ones, such as camps that have specialties such as baroque music or chamber orchestras.

☞ Surf the web. Using a search engine such as Google, type in your interest plus the words *summer camp*, for example, biology + summer camp + high school. See if the search results give you any leads.

☞ Visit college websites. Many schools run their own summer enrichment programs, while others are administered by outside vendors who rent their dorms and facilities. It's not that an outside group can't offer a good program, but you want to know who's in charge and their credentials. Be sure and do a thorough reference check.

☞ Read newspaper educational supplements (for example, *The New York Times* publishes two major education supplements each year) for articles and ads on summer academic programs.

☞ Search guides such as *Peterson's Summer Opportunities for Kids and Teenagers* for information on summer programs and travel opportunities.

Athletes in the Summer

If you are serious about playing a varsity sport in college, you will have to continue your training throughout the summer. That would mean scheduling any physical workouts that you need, taking lessons if appropriate, plus attending at least one or two sports camps (generally run as one-week sessions). You'll also want to play on an elite team (not associated with your high school). See Chapter 2 for more details on what you need to do during your summers to enhance your potential as an athletic recruit. But also make time to do some volunteer work or academics or hold some type of job during the summer—you should be more than whatever sport you play.

Working for Pay

One of the most productive activities you can do over the summer is to get a job, preferably for pay. As Goucher College Director of Admissions Surbeck explains, "I'll always believe that the student who works gains a greater understanding of what it takes to go to college."

Entering the workforce teaches you about responsibility, punctuality, reliability, and teamwork. You also learn discipline, communication, and interpersonal skills, and you may have a chance to show your initiative and creativity. A job can give you a sneak peek into some career paths—and possibly give you some insight into the kinds of jobs you *don't* want to do. For example, one student spent his vacation working on Wall Street in a low-level clerical job. Those three months were enough to convince him that he did not want to work in the financial district in the future. That's a valuable lesson, too.

On the other hand, even if it's a job that totally bores you, it can teach you something important. One student wrote his college essay about the summer he spent working for a dry-cleaning store. The time spent with an immigrant family, who devoted countless hours to their small business and who drew upon their extended family to support the enterprise, taught this student some important life lessons, which he shared in his application.

Even if you have to have a paying job, Rory Shaffer, director of admissions at Adelphi University, Garden City, New York, suggests, "We all know that students have to work for the most part, but in their spare time they should develop and explore their areas of interest. If they are interested in art, they should paint, if they want to teach, they need to do volunteer teaching."

Plan Ahead

If you want to get a paying job, you need to develop some marketable skills. You can look for the more traditional teen jobs—baby-sitter, counselor, lawn worker—but with a little advance planning and legwork, you might be able to snag a better-paying job. For example, if you are computer-literate, your worth to an office looking for temporary summer help may be significantly higher. Besides word processing (which you absolutely must be comfortable doing long before you go to college), it's helpful if you know desktop publishing, web design, and spreadsheet and analysis programs. Some high schools and community colleges offer Cisco certification programs, in which students learn how to design, build, and maintain computer networks. You can expect a significantly higher-paying job if you are Cisco-certified.

The more skills you can offer, the better your chances of finding a good-paying job. But that means you should get any certification you will need (or take any necessary refresher classes) the spring before you look for a job. For example, the winter before, check on when the Red Cross is offering lifeguard certification in your area. You can expect to receive almost double the pay a camp counselor receives just because you took a few weeks to get your lifeguard certification. Add in a water safety instructor badge, and you increase your value even more.

The spring is also the time to practice various computer programs so you can handle any tests that a prospective employer might ask you to take during an interview.

Resumé Smarts

Your job hunting will be easier if you create a resumé that tells prospective employers the skills you have to offer. In addition to your name, address, telephone number, and e-mail address, be sure to include any experience you have (this can include work experience you gained through your volunteer work). For example, if you are looking for a job in desktop publishing, and you've been part of the layout and design team on your high school newspaper, include that on your resumé. If you are looking for a job as a camp counselor, include any volunteer work you've done with your house of worship youth group or Sunday School.

See the following sample resumé for more ideas of what to include on your resumé.

Sarah Student
1234 Any Street
Anywhere, MI 12345
555-123-4567
sstudent@earth.com

Education:	Junior, Truman High School, Anywhere, MI
GPA:	3.8 on a 4.0 scale
	Member, National Honor Society
Experience:	2000–2002 *Truman High School Newspaper*
	Currently, news editor. Responsible for developing editorial lineup, assigning articles, editing copy, making revisions, writing headlines, and laying out and designing the front page.
	I will be editor-in-chief for the upcoming school year, responsible for the overall production and design of the monthly school newspaper.
	2000–2002 *Truman High School Literary Magazine*
	Began as contributor in freshman year; currently poetry editor of the bi-monthly publication.
Office Skills:	Proficient in Microsoft Word, Excel, Publisher, and Power Point

Where to Find Jobs

It's hard for anyone to find a job in a tight economy, but for teens, it's always more difficult. You can find the more traditional teen jobs through your youth employment service, guidance office, or the Yellow Pages (check under "Day Camps"), but you should also check out newspaper ads, office temp businesses, and college and community bulletin boards.

Don't forget to wear out a little shoe leather. Walk into local businesses offices and private clubs and ask if they have any openings for summer help. Offer to begin, on a part-time basis, before the season starts (but keep in mind that you shouldn't take away important study time during finals).

No matter how well done, a resumé is a piece of paper, and sometimes one of many an employer receives. Personal contact can make you stand out from the crowd—and get you the job.

It's also reasonable to ask family friends and your friends' parents for a job. That's the reality of the job world. But you should still create a resumé and look for a job on your own as well. Trying to land a job is a learning experience in and of itself.

Create Your Own Job

If you can't find a job that interests you, you might consider creating your own work. Take the same skills you have and approach local businesses or individuals with a business plan. For example, if you are proficient in desktop publishing, create sample brochures and flyers. A local hardware store may be interested in doing a mailing to promote a sale or store event. It's unlikely that you will get business from a national chain store, but local businesses often need help and may be more apt to help you out.

Other jobs, especially for younger teens, might include a cleaning service, pet-sitting, yard work, errand service, tutoring, catering, or painting. Give yourself a clever name and advertise your services by word of mouth, bulletin boards, or brochures distributed throughout your neighborhood. One group of teens created Bowties, a party helper service. They built the business slowly, primarily through word of mouth, but at the end of their third year in business, they could include on their college applications the story of the business, how it had grown over three years, and how it had been expanded to include hiring additional help to handle more sophisticated parties. This kind of experience showed colleges the resourcefulness, initiative, and creativity of the applicants.

Bottom line: Getting a job shows colleges that you aren't afraid of hard work and that you are responsible and realistic—even creative and flexible. These are the kinds of characteristics that help a student succeed in college—and in life.

Volunteer Work Is Valuable

As covered in Chapter 3, volunteering in some type of service activity is good in many ways. You should volunteer because it makes you a better person. But yes, it also gives colleges insight into another side of you. As Surbeck points out, "Some of the best accounts of students maturing have come from summer community service endeavors."

Besides, the skills you learn from a volunteer job can be as educational as anything you learn in a classroom. Working in a nursing home, for example, develops your interpersonal skills, gives you insight into the aging process, makes you practice time management, and encourages your empathy and compassion.

Summertime is a great time to volunteer because you have more free time and the opportunities to work may be greater. Some high schools even require a certain amount of community service in order to graduate. Summer vacation may be the ideal time to complete this prerequisite, especially if you are very busy with schoolwork and other extracurricular activities during the regular school year.

If you have been volunteering during the school year, you may wish to continue during your summer vacation. In fact, it may be of greater help to the organization if you fill in for vacationing employees during the summer. But you may want to explore other opportunities, perhaps some outside your community. Several organizations seek older teens as volunteers, for example:

✏ Habitat for Humanity has national and international placements in building homes for the needy. You may want to join this program as part of a youth group from your house of worship. There are fees to participate.

- The Student Conservation Association has national placements for teens interested in the environment. Students 15 and older are assigned to work crews focusing on environmental and restoration projects.

- Volunteers for Peace have a limited number of international placements for teens over age 15 who are interested in promoting world peace.

- Landmark Volunteers places students over age 15 in programs at historic trust sites throughout the United States.

To find an interesting, out-of-community volunteer opportunity, check with your guidance counselor, search the web, or consult a private camp advisor. Remember, many volunteer opportunities cost money to participate, so although you will be doing worthwhile work, you need to consult with your parents before enrolling. They need to make sure that the project is safe, the supervision is reasonable, and the cost is not prohibitive.

Although an international placement may sound exciting, every community has a need for volunteers, and in a tight economy, service organizations frequently are the hardest hit. So be sure see if your volunteer service can't be put to good use closer to home. Here are some places to start looking:

- Local hospitals
- Ambulance corps
- Firehouse
- Homeless shelters and soup kitchens
- Literacy programs
- Nursing homes
- Day-care centers
- Environmental groups
- Animal shelters

Travel and Teen Tours

Travel is broadening, and teen tours are a way of seeing new places in the company of peers. There are lots of tour options, some of which are primarily sightseeing, but others involve some kind of physical challenge (for example, bike tours, camping, spelunking, wind surfing, and rock climbing, just to name a few). You can learn valuable lessons from these travel opportunities, and the knowledge you gain will prove helpful when applying to college.

Besides visiting different parts of the country or globe, teen tours also give you an opportunity to …

- Travel independently (or at least, more independently than traveling with your family). You will need to know how to do this when you leave for college.

- Shoulder responsibility for your own belongings, and on some programs, handle cooking, cleanup, laundry, etc. Becoming responsible for your own well-being is critical to successfully living on your own in college and beyond.

- Build your self-esteem, since completing challenging physical programs can be very satisfying. Believing in your own abilities will be critical through the college application process, as well as through your freshman year.

- Learn teamwork. Group dynamics and cooperation are critical for a successful trip. Knowing how to negotiate living and working with a group will be important when you live in a college dorm, play a varsity team sport, or simply contribute to college life as an active member of the community.

Bottom line: Travel can be an educational and challenging experience that provides you with skills that will prove helpful in your transition to college.

Reference Checks

Whether you opt for a teen tour, an academic program, or work at a camp, you and your parents need to do a thorough reference check to make sure that the activity is safe and as good as the marketing material purports.

- ☞ Make sure the references are recent. The leadership of the program may have changed over time so you want to be sure that the information you get about the activity is current.

- ☞ While your parents need to do a separate reference check about safety, supervision, money matters, meals, insurance, etc., you will want to talk to teens who have actually participated in the program you are interested in attending. You'll need another student's input on living conditions, level of instruction, responsibilities, food, free time, etc.

Before the Summer Ends

At the close of whatever program, volunteer service, or job you have, talk to your immediate supervisor or teacher and ask if you may use him as a reference in the future. Ask for his addresses—e-mail and snail mail—so you can keep in touch. You may want to return to the program/job at some other point, or you may want to ask for a letter of recommendation when you apply to colleges. This type of letter is valuable because it tells colleges about a different side of you. A job supervisor can describe qualities about you that a teacher may not know.

Before you return to school, write a note to your supervisor. Thank him for the opportunity to work, tell him how much you learned over the summer, and say you will stay in touch.

At the holiday time, send a greeting card, noting how much you enjoyed the previous summer.

These are all accepted business practices to let employers (and supervisors) know how much you appreciated their efforts. It will make a difference when they are looking for someone to hire or when you ask them for a letter of reference.

Add to Your College Box

At the end of each summer, summarize what you did. Be sure and include your exact responsibilities, the name and address of your supervisor, and your impressions of what you learned. Noting this information while it's fresh in your mind will make it easier for you to recall specifics when you are completing your applications.

What You Need to Know

- Use your summer vacations to challenge yourself.
- Working for pay shows colleges that you are responsible, disciplined, and realistic.
- Use your initiative and skills to create your own job if you can't find one.
- Spend the summer exploring several different activities: working with academics, performing community service, or traveling.

Chapter 5

The Inside Scoop on Standardized Testing

Coming Up in This Chapter

- The SAT I test: controversial, demanding, and challenging—but still the most widely used college entrance examination
- All students need to prepare for standardized testing—the only question is how
- What you can learn from the PSAT/NMSQT, a preview of the SAT I
- Is the ACT right for you?

Do the acronyms SAT I and SAT II strike terror in your heart? How about PSAT/NMSQT? Does ACT?

Although you've been taking standardized exams since you entered kindergarten (and perhaps before if you were applying to some private schools), testing takes on a whole new meaning in the college application process. In this chapter I'll go over all the tests (optional and mandatory) you need to take in high school, when to take them, what the scores mean, how to prepare for them, and the lowdown on prep courses.

Even if you think you are a terrible test-taker, I'll talk about your options—which include looking for schools that think standardized tests are meaningless.

Some Definitions

ACT   Pronounced *A-C-T,* this standardized test measures English, math, reading, and science reasoning and is used by some colleges as part of admissions prerequisite.

College Board   This nonprofit organization owns various standardized tests, including PSAT, SAT I, SAT II, and AP exams.

Educational Testing Service   This national organization focuses on educational testing and research. It is responsible for designing and administering the College Board tests.

PSAT/NMSQT   The Preliminary SAT/National Merit Scholarship Qualifying Test is more commonly known as the PSAT. It may be taken as practice in ninth and tenth grades, but results count for entry into National Merit competitions only when taken in junior year. According to the College Board, the PSAT/NMSQT measures verbal reasoning skills, critical reading skills, math problem-solving skills, and writing skills.

SAT I   Pronounced *S-A-T,* this standardized test measures verbal skills and mathematical problem-solving. It is normally taken once in spring of junior year and again, if necessary, in senior year. Some students take the exam in January of their junior year, with a second attempt in May or June, which still leaves an option of a third and final attempt in October of their senior year.

SAT II   Subject Tests (formerly called Achievement Tests), these multiple-choice tests are designed to measure your knowledge or skills in a particular subject, for example history or biology.

SAT I

When to take: Junior year and again in senior year if necessary. Some students take the exam in January of their junior year and again, if necessary, in May or June of that same year. That leaves October of their senior year for a third attempt, if they are still concerned about their score.

Where to enroll: Sign up online (www.collegeboard.com), over the phone, if you have previously registered for any College Board exam

(1-800-SAT-SCORE), or by mail directly with the College Board (get a registration bulletin from your counselor).

Fee: $25, with an additional fee charged if you register late. Fee waivers are available for low-income students; check with your guidance counselor for more information. Fees are subject to change.

How long: 3 hours.

A Little History, a Lot of Controversy

The SAT I, the most widely administered college-entrance examination, is under attack—and not just by students who feel like their entire future is based on the scores of a three-hour test. Educational leaders question the content of the SAT I as well as its value as predictive of collegiate success. Richard C. Atkinson, president of the nine-campus University of California system, has proposed eliminating the SAT I requirement for applicants. How did a three-hour test become so powerful? And is its reign about to end?

What's in a Name?

Some critics say it's all just window dressing, but the name changes the SAT has undergone reflect an attempt to alter the public perception of just what the test measures. It was first called the Scholastic Aptitude Test, and the idea was that it measured how innately smart you were. Then in 1994, it changed its name to the Scholastic Assessment Test, suggesting that it was measuring your academic achievement. By the late 1990s, SAT was no longer an abbreviation, but, in fact, the name of the test. It is pronounced S-A-T.

The SAT, first administered in 1926, is a test originally designed to measure innate mental ability—in other words, it was an IQ test. It became widely used in the 1940s and 1950s, due in large measure to then president of Harvard University, James B. Conant. Conant believed that the SAT would level the playing field between the privileged, moneyed elite who attended private prep schools and the less economically advantaged who attended public schools. The leaders of the future would earn their spots because of their brains, not because of inheritance or family name. Test researchers claimed that admission officers could use SAT results to predict how well students would do in their freshman year of college. Wow! No wonder admissions officers loved the test. They believed that the higher the score, the better the student would do academically in college. And the fact that there was no direct correlation between what the SAT I tested and what a student learned in school was dismissed as irrelevant.

Was there really a correlation between SAT I success and freshman grades? According to a study of 78,000 first-year University of California students, no. Researchers compared three variables to freshman success: high school grades, SAT I scores, and SAT II (Subject Tests) scores. The greatest predictor of how well a student would do in the first year of college? Scores on SAT II tests. The second best predictor? High school grades. Test scores from the SAT I were the least useful. As University of California president Atkinson argues, "Achievement tests are fairer to students because they measure accomplishment rather than promise." SAT II tests assess what you actually learned, not what your potential might be.

Some claim that the SAT I can be used to compare students from different schools. In other words, if a college admissions officer didn't know the academic rigor of a high school, he could use the standardized test scores of applicants as a means of comparison. But this theory may be in question based on a study of applicants to the Texas state university system.

Since 1997, the University of Texas has admitted any student in the top 10 percent of his class, regardless of his SAT I scores. That means that the top students from both academically demanding high schools as well as those from marginal schools are all admitted to the university.

How did those students from less academically demanding high schools fare? A recent analysis revealed that the "top 10 percenters" get excellent grades as college freshmen, regardless of which high school they attended. These students are faring as well as students who got SAT scores that are 200 to 300 points higher. If you think about it, it makes sense. The effort and determination necessary to get good grades is every bit as important as abilities, if not more so.

One of the biggest criticisms of the SAT I is the huge performance gap between students of different races. White students score significantly higher than black and Hispanic students. Some experts believe that the test questions have an inherent bias that assumes a white, middle-class culture. Others suggest that the gap is a result of economic and cultural differences, with more blacks and Hispanics attending poorer schools and not getting the essential education in math and reading that produces better scores. Whatever the reasons, the problem persists and adds fuel to the SAT debate.

According to Jeff Rubenstein, assistant vice president for program development of The Princeton Review, a test prep company, the SAT I doesn't test for intelligence or for knowledge of what is taught in school. Instead, the results only show "that very narrow skill of how you do on the SAT." Rubenstein is especially critical of the math section, "which has no strong relationship to real math. You can be very good at math but still bomb the SAT."

Bottom line: Many people have concluded that the SAT I test is a flawed test, and it will probably lose some of its significance in terms of college admissions in the next 10 years (if not sooner). But if you are going to apply to a school that requires the test, it's still better to get the highest score you can get—and that takes some work.

Some Schools Say No to SATs

Some colleges don't require the SAT I exam as part of their application process. For 17 years, Bates College, Lewiston, Maine, a top-ranked liberal arts college, has given applicants the option of not taking standardized tests—neither the SAT I nor SAT II. Bates believes that the information the school gleans from an applicant's transcript, essay, extracurricular activities, and recommendations tells them all they need to know about the student—and far more than standardized test numbers could. In an article in *The Chronicle of Higher Education*, William C. Hiss, Bates vice president for external and alumni affairs, makes a strong case. He points out that the school has carefully tracked the grade point averages and graduation rates of students, both those who choose to submit their scores and the one quarter to one third of incoming students who opted not to submit test results. The GPAs and graduation rates were nearly identical between the two groups.

Hiss argues that the Bates applicant pool has grown significantly since eliminating the SAT requirement, without diluting quality, because Bates's "no SAT" option encourages strong students who are poor test-takers to apply.

Bottom line: Many colleges have made submitting standardized test scores optional. If you are concerned that your scores will be a problem, you should consider those schools who don't place a high importance on standardized test scores. You may prefer a school that thinks beyond the numbers. But on the other hand, don't limit yourself only to schools that opted out of the SAT game. Most colleges stress that, in any case, SAT scores are just one small part of the application process.

SAT Stats

According to a study published in *The Chronicle of Higher Education:*

- 1.3 million high school seniors take the SAT each year.
- More than half of high school seniors take the test at least twice (in their junior and senior years).
- 45 percent of all high school seniors take the test.

What's on the SAT I?

There are two parts to the SAT I: verbal and math.

In the verbal section, you will find …

- Nineteen analogy questions, which test your knowledge of word meanings, how well you see relationships in a pair of words, and your ability to recognize a similar or parallel relationship.

✏ Nineteen sentence-completion questions, which assess how much you know about the meaning of words and how different parts of a sentence fit together.

✏ Forty critical reading questions, which focus on your ability to think carefully and critically about a passage or a pair of related passages.

In the math section, you will find …

✏ Thirty-five multiple-choice questions, for which you decide which is the best of the five choices given.

✏ Fifteen four-choice quantitative comparison questions, for which you are given two quantities to compare and choose the best answer from the four choices given.

✏ Ten student-produced response (grid-ins) questions for which you solve the problem and grid in the answer.

What Gives Students an Edge in the SAT I Game?

The Princeton Review's Jeff Rubenstein believes that students who enjoy puzzles like crossword puzzles, acrostics, jumbles, or math teasers tend to do better at the SATs because that is the underlying premise of the test. If you remember that it's not a test of school-educated math or verbal knowledge, you can see that having an aptitude for puzzles may be an advantage.

Rubenstein and other test-prep experts (and even the College Board) say that students who enjoy reading have a special advantage when taking the SATs. You can't make up in any prep course the language skills you acquire if you read widely over several years.

SAT Preparation: What You Need to Know

Everyone needs to prepare for the SAT I exam. For this test, it's not a question of just keeping up with your studies to get a good score. There are "tricks of the trade," or strategies, that can mean the difference between a good score and a great score. To name just a few …

- Knowing how to eliminate answers in a multiple-choice question.
- Understanding in what order the questions on the SAT are posed.
- Appreciating the value of guessing.
- Being clear on the points you get for a right answer, a wrong answer, and a blank answer.

Even the College Board, which questions the value of hard-core SAT tutoring, has an extensive website (www.collegeboard.com) devoted to understanding the tests, offering practice exams, providing tips, and more.

Bottom line: The issue is not whether or not you need SAT prep; it's how you're going to get it. According to Rubenstein, "You get out of test prep what you put into it." You need to make a commitment to preparing for the SATs if you hope to get a good score. As Stanley Kaplan, founder of Kaplan, Inc., a test-prep company, writes in his memoir, *Test Pilot: How I Broke Testing Barriers for Millions of Students and Caused a Sonic Boom in the Business of Education*, "Acquiring test-taking skills is the same as learning to play the piano or riding a bicycle. It requires practice, practice, practice. Repetition breeds familiarity. Familiarity breeds confidence."

One-on-One, Classes, or Online?

Will you take an SAT course, hire a private tutor, or study for the exam on your own? The only answer is that it's up to you and your parents. There's money involved—a substantial amount of money if you hire a tutor or enroll in a program—so you need to consider money and your motivation before you make a decision. As Richard Bavaria, vice president of education for Sylvan Learning Centers, a national test-prep company, explains, "No two kids think and learn alike. Everyone needs to prepare for these tests, but the kind of preparation will vary from test-taker to test-taker."

To find out what kind of test-prep is right for you, answer these questions:

- Will you feel more comfortable, and will you make the time commitment you need, if you take an SAT-prep course?

☞ Does your learning style and schedule permit you to enroll in a course, or do you need to arrange for private tutoring?

If you decide that you can't prepare for the SAT I on your own, you have several options:

☞ You can hire a private tutor or even two (one for math skills and one for verbal) and tailor the tutoring sessions to your schedule. This can be convenient if you can afford it. Private tutoring is also helpful if you need to focus more on one or the other subject—for example, your math skills are fine, but you really need help with the verbal section. Private tutoring may also help if you have physical or learning disabilities and need to have SAT prep adapted to your particular learning style.

☞ If you prefer a classroom atmosphere, with the peer support and the consistency of regularly scheduled classes and practice exams, you can enroll in a class. Your high school or adult-education program may offer classes. If you go to the websites of the national chains (for example, The Princeton Review, Kaplan, or Sylvan Learning Center), you can type in your address to find out when and where classes are available near you.

☞ You can take classes online, either self-instructed or in virtual classroom with a live instructor. This works if you can't find a local tutor or if the larger classes either don't appeal to you or don't fit into your time schedule.

All these options cost money.

☞ The price will vary depending on where you live, but the national chains charge almost $1,000 for 35 hours of instruction plus 14 hours of practice test-taking (in classes that have 12 students on average).

☞ Private tutors range from $50 to $150 per hour. In New York City, some tutors charge as much as $200 to $450 or even $500 an hour.

☞ Publicly funded classes offered by your local high school or library can still cost several hundred dollars.

☞ Online classes range from $400 (for 20 self-taught lessons) to $800 for a live instructor in a virtual classroom with seven other students logged on at the same time.

On Your Own

There are plenty of good SAT-prep books on the market, including some by the leading national companies that offer SAT prep, which can help you learn the "tricks" of taking the SATs. There are even websites devoted to the topics. (See Appendix A for a list of helpful books and websites.)

But if you decide to teach yourself, you have to be motivated to do the work—seriously motivated. An SAT-prep course given by The Princeton Review consists of 35 hours of instruction and 14 hours of practice test-taking. That's a huge time commitment you have to carve out of your schedule. It's certainly easier to sign up for a course and build it into your workweek than trying to teach yourself. The reasoning: You or your parents have paid big bucks for the class, so you have to show up. But if you are intent on preparing for the SAT on your own, you have to make that time in your week just as if you were walking into a classroom somewhere.

Plus, you have to know your own capabilities:

- Are you comfortable taking tests? Do you tend to get nervous and never quite relax when confronted with an exam?
- Do you usually do well on tests?
- Did you do well on the PSAT? Combining the math and verbal sections, not the writing skills sections, did you get a score over 130? That would suggest that you would score at least a 1300 on the SAT I. You can assume that your score will probably go up because, on average, scores rise with each successive test—as you become more familiar with the exam and complete more coursework, you become more proficient.
- Have you ever taught yourself any other subject? Most people find it easier to learn from an experienced teacher who can put the technical jargon into layman's terms.
- Do you find it easier to learn with fellow students? It can be more interesting—and even more fun—to share this experience with someone else who is going through the same process. Plus you can learn from each other.

Let's Talk Honestly About Your SAT I Scores

Your SAT I will be a combination of one score for verbal and one for math, which combine to give you a score in a range from 200 (the lowest) to 800 (the highest). The average score, according to the Educational Testing Service, is 1020, reflecting 506 on verbal, 514 on math. But student scores are calculated in the "tens," so you would never receive a 506 or 514, but rather a 510 and 520.

A perfect score is 1600, but less than 1 percent of all students who take the exam each year receive that perfect score. And don't get carried away—even if you get a perfect score, that's not a sure pass into a top college! In fact, it can be a drawback (more on that later!).

Scoring on the SAT I is a little tricky. Here's why. Unlike the ACT exam (see later in this chapter), you are penalized for wrong answers on the SATs. For every right answer you get one point, for every omitted question you get no point, and for every wrong answer, you lose a fraction of a point. For a wrong answer on a five-choice question, or questions with five answer choices, you lose $1/4$ point, and $1/3$ point is subtracted for a wrong answer on a four-choice question, or question with four answer choices. So if there are 35 questions in one section, let's say you answer 30 of them correctly and leave 5 of them blank. Your score for that section would be 30. Now let's assume you answer 30 correctly and make educated guesses on the answers for the remaining 5. You get three correct but miss one five-choice question and one four-choice question. Your score under those circumstances would be 33 ($33 - 1/4$ point $- 1/3$ point, which is then rounded up to the nearest whole number). If you can make reasonably educated guesses, it will be worth it to you to take the chance.

But what do you need to know about the scores? Obviously the higher they are, the better. When you are deciding on which schools interest you, read their material, check out their website, peruse the various rankings, and also note what the average SATs of incoming freshmen are.

For example, for the 2004 class at Carleton College, Northfield, Minnesota, here is the range of SAT I test scores (as reported on the college's website):

Math:

- 1 percent had scores below 500.
- 2 percent had scores between 500 and 549.
- 5 percent had scores between 550 and 599.
- 17 percent had scores between 600 and 649.
- 27 percent had scores between 650 and 699.
- 20 percent had scores between 700 and 749.
- 14 percent had scores between 750 and 800.
- 14 percent didn't take the SAT I.

Verbal:

- 1 percent had scores below 500.
- 2 percent had scores between 500 and 549.
- 6 percent had scores between 550 and 599.
- 13 percent had scores between 600 and 649.
- 18 percent had scores between 650 and 699.
- 22 percent had scores between 700 and 749.
- 24 percent had scores between 750 and 800.
- 14 percent didn't take the SAT I.

Some students had scores that were very low, while others aced the test, but the average student probably had scores in the 1300s.

What's the Minimum?

According to Rubenstein at The Princeton Review, if you have a combined score of 1150 on your SAT I, your board scores are just fine for most competitive colleges. For the Ivy Leagues and the most competitive colleges, you'll need at least 1350.

If your scores are significantly lower than the average score, the other parts of your application better be strong. Low SAT I scores may not be a deal-breaker. If your GPA is high, your activities strong, and your essay thoughtful, it's easy for an admissions officer to say "This is just a kid who isn't particularly good at standardized tests."

If your scores are significantly higher than the average, there are two important points to remember:

- If you have very high SAT scores but your high school grades are less than stellar, you've got some explaining to do. Every admissions officer in the country is going to ask why you did so well on the SATs but didn't focus on your schoolwork. It shows you are not living up to your potential—and no college likes that.

- If your grades meet the average GPA of incoming freshmen and your SATs are significantly higher, you may be in a stronger position. You may be more interesting to a college admissions officer because you raise their average SAT score—and that boosts the college's profile (and helps raise the institution's standing in the national rankings of colleges). Further, you may be eligible for special merit scholarships at certain colleges. For example, the University of Rochester, New York, offers Rush Rhees Scholarships to entering freshmen on the basis of academic excellence, including standardized test scores on the SAT I or ACT, as well as comparable academic performance. These are merit scholarships that are awarded on the basis of outstanding academic performance, not financial need, and are worth $5,000 for New York residents and generally $10,000 for out-of-state students. In recent years, applicants needed a minimum of 1250 on their SAT I exam to be eligible for this award.

Bottom line: For most colleges, SAT I scores won't get you in to college but also won't keep you out, assuming your score is around the average stated in their student profile. A really high score coupled with a low GPA is a tip-off to college admissions officers that you are not working as hard as you should. But a lower score for someone with a high GPA may not be an obstacle to admission.

Should You Take Them Again?

If you are disappointed in your test scores, you can always take them again. If you took the exam in May or June of your junior year, you can still take the test in October, November, or December of your senior year.

If you are applying early decision, you can pay a premium to rush the scores to the college of your choice to be included in your folder. Rushing scores doesn't speed reporting for the current test. Scores are all reported at the same time. Rushing is only useful for sending scores of previous tests. Colleges look at the scores and record the highest verbal score achieved and the highest math score achieved, even if they are from two different tests.

For example, let's say on the May test, you scored a 580 on your verbal and a 610 on your math (for a combined score of 1190). You decide to retake the test in October, and this time you score a 620 on your verbal but only a 600 on your math (for a combined score of 1220). Most college admissions officers will consider the higher verbal score from the October test but will refer to the higher math score from the May test—giving you a combined score of 1230. Not much of a leap, but it is a slight improvement.

Score Range

Colleges understand about score range and that on any given day, a student might score 30 points higher or lower per section. For example, a student who scores 660 on the verbal section of the SAT I could be expected to score anywhere from 630 to 690 on the section if they were to take it again immediately. That's because a host of factors can affect a student's performance. He might be feeling sick so his score is lower or, conversely, he's feeling fine and just happened to hit a verbal section that had all the words he studied the week before the exam so his score is higher. The same thing could happen on the math section.

If you take the test more than once, all SAT I test results will be reported to the colleges and scholarship programs you designate.

Remember: Don't get suckered into thinking that you need to hit your SAT scores out of the ballpark and keep retaking the test in a vain attempt to raise your scores. The difference between a 1350 and a 1410 isn't significant. And at least half of those who score a perfect 1600 are rejected at Harvard. I'm convinced that there is almost a perverse glee that admissions officers get in rejecting an applicant with a perfect SAT score. It shows the college is looking beyond the numbers!

The PSAT/NMSQT

When to take: Sophomore year for practice or junior year to be considered for scholarship and recognition programs.

Where to enroll: In your high school guidance office.

Fee: $9.50 (although some schools charge additional administration fee). Fee waivers are available for low-income students. Check with your guidance counselor for more information. Fees are subject to change.

How long: 2 hours, 10 minutes.

The Preliminary SAT/National Merit Scholarship Qualifying Test is co-sponsored by the College Board and the National Merit Scholarship Corporation (NMSC). Students take the exam in the fall of their junior year, but some schools encourage sophomores to take the PSAT as a practice exercise.

You register for the exam with your guidance counselor (as opposed to the SATs, where you register directly with ETS). The test results are reported to you via your high school, in contrast to the SATs, which are mailed directly to your home. Test scores are not released to colleges, and even if you choose to send them, they are not included in the decision-making process. (Top-scoring students do have the option of having the NMSC send their scores to two colleges; see the following section for more details.)

The purposes of the PSAT are as follows:

- To give you practice on a SAT-like test. The PSAT includes actual SAT questions.
- To serve as a preview of your performance on the SAT I. You'll establish your baseline score on a standardized test.
- To get feedback to improve your skills. The Score Report Plus is personalized to help you improve your skills.
- To participate, if you choose, in the Student Search Service. This service lets colleges know you are interested in hearing from them—be prepared for lots of mail!

❏ To enter National Merit Scholarship Corporation scholarship competitions. You must take the PSAT in your junior year to be eligible for National Merit scholarships.

The test requires 2 hours, 10 minutes and is made up of the following:

❏ Two 25-minute verbal sections

❏ Two 25-minute math sections

❏ One 30-minute writing skills section

PSAT Particulars

Verbal Sections

There are 52 questions in the two verbal sections of the test: 13 sentence completions, 13 analogies, and 26 critical reading questions. (See the earlier "What's on the SAT I?" section for an explanation of each type of question.)

Math Sections

There are 40 questions in the two math sections: 20 regular multiple choice, 12 quantitative comparisons, and 8 student-produced responses (also called grid-ins). *Bring a calculator.* Although, theoretically, no question on the test requires a calculator, it will help you, especially in the student-produced response section. And although you need a basic knowledge of arithmetic, algebra, and geometry, you don't need to have taken a full year of geometry.

Writing Skills Section

There are 39 questions in this one 30-minute section: 19 identifying sentence errors, 14 improving sentences, and 6 improving paragraph questions. According to the College Board, identifying sentence errors questions "test your knowledge of grammar, usage, word choice, and idiom. You are required to find errors in sentences or indicate that there is no error." Improving sentences questions "ask you to choose the best, most effective form of an underlined portion of a given sentence." Improving paragraphs questions "require you to make choices about improving the logic, coherence, or organization in a flawed passage."

Your PSAT Scores and Awards

The PSAT is scored on a 20 to 80 range. Because the SATs are graded from 200 to 800, all you have to do is add a zero to your math and verbal PSAT scores to get a comparison between the tests.

Your PSAT scores are for you only and can serve as guide to what you need to focus on in preparation for the SATs. If you aced the math section but didn't do as well on the verbal, you might want to focus most of your SAT I–prep efforts on the verbal section.

The exception is if you did extremely well on the PSAT. The very top scorers are recognized for their achievements. Each year approximately 1.2 million students take the exam. Of that, about 50,000 with the highest scores (verbal + math + writing skills) will qualify for recognition. Here's how it works:

- ➻ You take the exam in the fall of your junior year and receive your score reports within six weeks.

- ➻ You are notified in the following April (still in your junior year), if you are one of the top scorers.

- ➻ You will be told, through your school, in September (now in your senior year) if you have qualified as either a Commended Student or a Semi-finalist. At this point, the process is still based strictly on numbers.

About 34,000 of the approximately 50,000 top scorers will receive Letters of Commendation. It's an honor and certainly should be included on any college application under the section listing all your awards and honors. If you receive a Letter of Commendation you are not eligible for any Merit Scholarship awards, but you may be a candidate for other scholarships sponsored by corporations and businesses.

The remaining 16,000 students are the very top scorers and will be notified that they are Semifinalists. Here's where it gets a little tricky. The scores necessary for recognition as a Semifinalist depend on which state you are from, because, as noted on the National Merit Scholarship Program website, "To ensure that academically able young people from all parts of the United States are included in this talent pool, Semifinalists are designated on a state representational basis." So you might need to score at least 215 (verbal + math + writing skills scores) in Connecticut to qualify as a semifinalist, but only need 205 in Iowa. The numbers will vary from year to year, depending on the test results of the applicant pool. One year a student would need at least a 215 to qualify, but the next year's group of students would need a minimum score of 216, because the test results were slightly higher. You should, of course, include Semifinalist recognition on your college applications.

To move from Semifinalist to Finalist and possibly Merit Scholarship Winner, you will need to submit a letter of recommendation from your high school (your guidance counselor or principal will provide it); your transcript demonstrating an outstanding academic record; and an essay that describes your activities, interests, and goals. You will also need to take a second qualifying test. Finalists are named in February (of your senior year), so you should notify any colleges, in a separate letter to be included in your application file, if you receive this honor. Merit Scholarship winners are chosen from the Finalist group based, according to the NMSC, "on their abilities, skills, and accomplishments."

Should You Be Tutored for the PSAT?

You need to make this decision in concert with your parents. Here are the arguments, pro and con:

Against tutoring:

- The PSAT doesn't really count. It gives you an idea on how you do on standardized tests, but why waste money on tutoring—especially if you don't even know if you need it. It's better to spend the time working on your schoolwork—that does count!

- If you do well and are named a Commended Student or even a Semifinalist, congratulations. That's helpful, but you still need all the other parts of the application package to work before this honor makes the difference in getting into college.

- Generally, your test scores will improve just by taking this type of exam again. So no matter how you do on your PSAT, your SAT exam results will probably improve from the experience.

Pro tutoring:

- Like the SATs, there are "tricks" to learn that can improve your PSAT score (see the section on SAT tutoring). Why not learn them earlier rather than later so you will be more proficient by the time you take your SATs?
- If you are not a good test-taker, you may need the extra time to become comfortable, especially with this kind of exam.
- If you do well on the PSAT, you may be eligible for scholarship awards.

Bottom line: The PSAT gives you an idea of how you will fare on the SAT I exam, which you may need to take for college. Don't get freaked out if you don't score as well as you hoped, though. You still have time to get tutoring (either on your own or professionally) so that you can do better on the SAT.

If you ace the test, good for you. It's a nice feather in your cap; however, it is not a one-way ticket into the college of your choice.

Students with Disabilities

Students with physical or learning disabilities can arrange for services and appropriate accommodations when taking any of the College Board tests, including the PSAT/NMSQT, SAT I and II, and AP. You only need to submit one Services for Students with Disabilities (SSD) Eligibility Form, which remains valid throughout your high school years.

Your counselor can help you through this process. Your parents will need to sign the SSD Eligibility Form. The College Board recommends that you submit your SSD Eligibility Form early, preferably the spring *before* the year you take your first College Board test. For example, if you plan on taking the PSAT in October of your junior year, you should submit the SSD Eligibility Form in the spring of your sophomore year.

The College Board offers two types of accommodations: those that require extended time administration for the test (extending the time a student has to complete the exam), and those that do not. As an example of an accommodation that can be made within standard timed conditions, a hearing-impaired student may have a sign language interpreter to translate test instructions. Or for a visually impaired student, he can have a larger-print test booklet and answer sheet—again within the framework of the standard timed conditions.

If necessary, and approved, students may take the test under extended-time conditions. For example, some students with disabilities have been approved to have four and a half hours to complete the normally three-hour SAT I. Even if you are approved for testing under extended-time conditions, you may still not complete all the questions. Remember: About 20 percent of students who take the College Board tests under standard conditions do not complete them—that's not unusual. Even if you leave some answers blank, you can still receive an above-average score.

Bottom line: If you have already been diagnosed with a learning or physical disability, talk to your guidance counselor about getting your Services for Students with Disabilities Eligibility Form completed and approved. You may need to meet with the high school counselor while you are still in eighth grade if you anticipate taking any SAT II subject tests at the end of ninth grade (see the next section on SAT II exams for a discussion on when to take these tests).

SAT II: Testing What You Know

When to take: As coursework is completed (see the following section for information on language tests).

Where to enroll: Register online (www.collegeboard.com), by telephone if you have previously registered for any College Board exam (1-800-SAT-SCORE), or by mail with ETS (get a registration bulletin from your counselor).

Fee: Add $14 basic fee to appropriate fee for each test: writing test: $11; language tests with listening: $8; all other subject tests: $6 each. Fee waivers are available for low-income students. See your guidance counselor for more information. Fees are subject to change.

How long: Each test is one hour.

Unlike the SAT I exam, SAT II tests (formerly called Achievement Tests) have escaped serious criticism because they measure what you know about a subject and your ability to apply that knowledge. In fact, some schools have eliminated the SAT I as part of their application requirements, but require applicants to submit SAT II scores. Many schools require both SAT I and SAT II results.

SAT II tests give colleges a better way to compare you to other students who have taken the same subject in high school; to determine your preparedness for different college programs; and to help in college course selection and, where appropriate, place you in higher-level college courses.

Except for the writing test, all other subject tests contain multiple-choice questions. The writing test is a combination of multiple-choice questions (40 minutes) and an essay that you have to write on an assigned topic (20 minutes).

Subject tests are given in the following:

- **English** (two tests): Writing and Literature
- **History** (two tests): U.S. History and World History
- **Mathematics** (two tests): Mathematics Level I C (calculator required for some questions) and Mathematics Level II C (calculator required for some questions)
- **Science** (three tests): Biology, Chemistry, Physics
- **Language** (13 tests): Chinese with Listening, French, French with Listening, German, German with Listening, Modern Hebrew, Italian, Japanese with Listening, Korean with Listening, Latin, Spanish, Spanish with Listening, and English Language Proficiency

When to Take the SAT II

If you feel that you have a good grasp of the material, you should take the subject test when you complete the course. For example, if you take biology in ninth grade, you should take the SAT II biology test in June. That way the material will still be fresh in your mind.

For language SAT II, wait until you have had at least three or even four complete years. Some middle schools begin language instruction in seventh grade but at a slower pace than a high school program. That means you complete one full year of instruction in seventh and eighth grade combined. In that case, wait until at least the end of your junior year before taking a language SAT II. If you are a native speaker of a language other than English, you can consider taking the test earlier. But remember that fluency doesn't necessarily prepare you for this type of test. The language tests involve listening and answering questions based on pictures, dialogs, and monologs; vocabulary and structure questions testing parts of speech and basic idioms, in sentences or longer paragraphs; as well as a reading comprehension section that contains questions based on passages drawn from fiction, essays, historical works, newspapers or magazine articles, and everyday materials such as advertisements, timetables, forms, and tickets. You may speak a language at home but not read or write the language. In that case, you may not want to take the SAT II.

How Many Tests to Take

On any given test day, you can take up to three SAT II exams. *But don't do it.* No matter how well you think you know the subjects, these tests can drain your energy and sharpness. You will be mighty tired at the end of the session if you do take three in one day. It's better to space them out, with no more than two at any one session.

If you have done well in a subject, take the SAT II exam. Obviously, if you have struggled throughout the year and your grades reflect those problems, skip the SAT II. Do try to include a least one science or math SAT II, as well as one in the humanities (history, English, or foreign language). Colleges want a balanced view of your abilities.

Many schools require the SAT II writing test and one other of your choice. But because you will take the exams as you finish the coursework, you may have several extra in your portfolio. That gives you some choice in which ones to send to colleges (see the following section for information on score choice).

SAT II Scores

The SAT II tests are scored from 200 to 800. But the average score is not 500; rather, it varies from test to test. Don't compare scores between different subject tests. Will your score improve if you take the test again? Maybe, if you continue to study the subject (this is especially true with language). And of course, there is some slight improvement likely just because you are more familiar with the kind of test; but then again, it might go down slightly, just because of question variations from test to test.

To give you an idea of how well you did, check out the average test scores for subject tests (from the College Board website):

- **English:** Writing: 595; Literature: 589
- **History:** U.S. History: 583; World History: 573
- **Mathematics:** Mathematics Level 1 C: 584; Mathematics Level II C: 663
- **Science:** Biology and Biology E/M: 584; Chemistry: 608; Physics: 640
- **Language:** Chinese with Listening: 748; French: 604; French with Listening: 625; German: 602; German with Listening: 605; Modern Hebrew: 593; Italian: 641; Japanese with Listening: 672; Korean with Listening: 746; Latin: 595; Spanish: 595; Spanish with Listening: 631; English Language Proficiency: 962 (scored on a scale of 901 to 999)

Score Choice: An Important Option That's Changing

All SAT I scores will appear on your permanent score report. Colleges can see how many times you took the test and your range of scores. Generally they consider your best score on each section, even if they are from different test dates.

But the SAT II subject tests are different. Currently you can choose which tests you want to be included on your permanent score report—but that is changing (see the following section).

Until then, however, the value of score choice is that you can decide, *after* you've seen your results, whether or not you want to release them to colleges. This gives you more control over what schools will see on your permanent record. Your results, under Score Choice, are reported only to you and your high school (if requested). Score Choice applies to *all* subject tests you take on any one exam day, *and* it cannot be elected *after* the test date. You must make this decision *before* the test.

This a more expensive option because, although it's free to have the scores released to your permanent record, you will have to pay later to have them sent to colleges or scholarship programs. The fee now is $6.50 for each college you choose to send your scores to if you notify ETS either online or by mail. If you telephone in your request, there is an additional $10 fee. There is also a surcharge if you rush your scores. (All fees are subject to change.)

If you don't elect Score Choice, your scores will be sent free of charge to the four colleges or scholarship programs you list (as part of your registration fee).

You can elect Score Choice in one of three ways:

- Fill in the Score Choice option on the registration form. *Do not* enter any college or scholarship programs on the registration form.
- Fill in the Score Choice option on the Correction Form and mail it in *before* the test date attached to your Admission Ticket.
- On the day of the test, complete the Score Choice option form. Ask the test supervisor for the form.

After you've received your test scores and have decided which scores you want to include, you can release the scores online, via regular mail, or by phone. Once you released the scores, you can't remove them from your permanent record.

Upcoming Changes in Score Choice

In December 2001, an advisory group of the College Board recommended the elimination of Score Choice for the following reasons:

- If colleges do indeed consider only the applicant's highest score, as the College Board clearly and emphatically encourages them to do, then Score Choice loses its importance and only increases anxiety.

- In schools where guidance counseling is insufficient, students do not always get accurate information. The demographics of the college-bound are changing, and in many respects, students are less affluent and less informed.

- Counselors have huge caseloads. To ask counselors to explain a change of an already-confusing policy to all students would be a difficult request to make. Furthermore, the process of changing the policy is extremely convoluted, and communicating the change to all stakeholders would be problematic.

- Score Choice entitles those who have access and encourages a sense of gamesmanship.

It's unclear when the College Board will eliminate Score Choice. First the organization believes it has to educate two groups: "(1) higher education professionals, in part by providing them with good information about what tests measure and how to use scores, and (2) the public, by asking higher education professionals and counselors to assist the College Board in quelling the public's frenetic mentality about scores and admissions."

It also appears that students who have already taken the Subject Tests will be "grandfathered," or permitted to keep their Score Choice option for those tests. Talk to your guidance counselor, who can tell you when the changes will take effect.

Bottom line: Score Choice is expensive but worth it for as long as it's available. It will give you a chance to review your scores and release those that make you look good. Elect Score Choice each time you take an SAT II subject test, then when you are ready to apply to colleges, review your scores and release those that you think are the best.

I Totally Blew It—Now What?

What happens if you get sick in the middle of the exam? Or if you open the test and wonder "What language is this?"—when the test is on English literature? In other words, what happens if you know, before you leave the test center, that you have totally and completely blown the test?

Well, if it's an SAT II test and you've elected Score Choice, it's not really a problem, because you'll see the results before they are released to your permanent record. If you're right and the score is 200 (which is what you get just for showing up), the score will never appear before an admissions officer's eyes.

But if you haven't chosen Score Choice—and you are certain you have bombed the SAT II test—you can cancel it—*but* you must do so almost immediately. If you know you want to cancel before you leave the room, ask the supervisor for a Request to Cancel Test Scores Form and complete it before leaving. If you get home and then decide, you must still act quickly. The College Board requires that they receive notice *in writing* by the Wednesday after the test. You can do so by e-mail, by fax, or by overnight mail delivery, and be sure to get some form of receipt confirmation.

Canceling the scores is an irrevocable process. You can't undo it, and it applies to *all* tests you took that day. So if you decide that you totally blew one of the subject tests but felt good about another, unfortunately, the cancellation applies to all scores for that test date. The only caveat: If your calculator dies during the Mathematics Subject Test or the cassette player for the Language Test with Listening malfunctions and you don't have backup equipment, you can cancel the score on the Mathematics Subject Test or the Language Test with Listening and still have your other subject tests scored.

Bottom line: Colleges are relying more on subject tests as a measure of a student's knowledge and breadth. You need to make sure that you have as much control as possible over what SAT II scores are submitted.

ACT: The Other Test

When to take: Junior year, again in your senior year if necessary.

Where to enroll: Sign up online (www.act.org), or by mail directly with the ACT (get a registration bulletin from your counselor). If you have previously taken an ACT test, you can reregister by telephone (1-800-525-6926).

Fee: $24 ($27 in Florida), plus an additional fee if registering late. Fee waivers are available for low-income students. Check with your guidance counselor for more information. Fees are subject to change.

How long: 3 hours and 30 minutes (including breaks).

The ACT is another college-entrance testing program, similar to the SAT. Like the SAT, the initials aren't an abbreviation for anything. It is pronounced *A-C-T.*

As a test, the ACT has come under less criticism than its ETS counterpart, primarily because it is more subject-related and, at least in theory, tests more of what you learn in school. Primarily public schools and schools in the middle of the country use it. In contrast, the SAT is used by more colleges and is preferred by private colleges and schools on the east and west coasts. While all the Ivy League colleges and virtually all U.S. colleges and universities accept the ACT, there is a caveat. For example, on The Princeton University website, the admissions office acknowledges "In those cases where the only other colleges to which a student is applying for admission are ones that require the ACT scores, we will accept the ACT scores in place of the SAT I scores (but not in place of the three required SAT II subject tests)."

Like the SAT, there are special provisions that can be made to accommodate students with disabilities (see your guidance counselor for more information). The issues about test preparation and tutors, as discussed earlier for the SAT, are similar, too.

The following table compares the SAT I exam to the ACT test.

The SAT vs. the ACT

	SAT I	ACT
Preferred by?	Private schools; schools on the east and west coasts	Public schools; schools in the middle of the country; more colleges than prefer the SAT I

continues

119

The SAT vs. the ACT *continued*

	SAT I	ACT
How questions appear	Order of difficulty	No order of difficulty
Score choice?	No	Yes
Highest math level	Algebra/basic geometry; test booklet supplies all formulas	Trigonometry (only four questions); test booklet rarely provides formulas
Skills heavily tested	Vocabulary and reading; math	Grammar and reading; math
Based on school curriculum?	Less	More
Penalty for wrong answers?	Yes	No
Style of test	Tricky, with many distracters	More straightforward, with distracters
Structure of test	Verbal: two 30-minute sections, one 15-minute section	English: one 45-minute section
	Math: two 30-minute sections, one 15-minute section	Math: one 60-minute section
	Experimental: one 30-minute verbal or math section; looks like any other section	Reading: one 35-minute section
		Science Reasoning: one 35-minute section
		Experimental: added to tests on certain dates; clearly added on

	SAT I	ACT
When it's offered	Seven times per year: late January, late March or early April, early May, early June, mid-October, early November, early December	Six times per year: February, April, June, September (in 13 states only), October, December
Scoring	200 to 800 for math and for verbal, added together for a composite score; median about 1000	1 to 36 for each subject, averaged together for a composite score; median about 21
When you should register	At least six weeks before the test date	At least four weeks before the test date
For more information	Educational Testing Service (ETS) www.act.org www.ets.org The College Board www.collegeboard.com	ACT 319-337-1000 609-771-7600

Reprinted with permission of The Princeton Review, www.review.com.

Bottom line: Check which test (SAT I or ACT), the school to which you're applying prefers. Don't take a test you don't need.

ACT Stats

- Taken by more than one million students.
- In 26 states, more students take the ACT than the SAT.
- Critics point out that there are gender and race differences in the median scores of ACT test-takers, similar to the criticisms faced by the SAT I.

Details on the ACT Test

The ACT test consists of four parts. On some tests, there is an additional experimental section. That section is clearly marked. The entire test has 215 multiple-choice questions.

- **English:** 45 minutes (The emphasis is on grammar.)
- **Math:** 60 minutes (The highest level of math included in the test is trigonometry, but there are only four trig questions. You may use a calculator—check the ACT website for which calculators are approved for use during the test.)
- **Reading:** 35 minutes
- **Science:** 35 minutes

ACT Scoring

Scoring for each section is 1 through 36, and then all four scores are averaged together for a composite score. The median score is 21. Scoring takes four to seven weeks after the test date, and there are no provisions for rushing the scores (which can be done for a fee with the SATs). If you take the test more than once, you may choose which date to release. You may list up to six colleges or scholarship programs to receive your score reports (in comparison to only four for the College Board tests) as part of your registration fee. The scores are released only by mail, unlike the SAT, where, for a fee, you can receive your scores by telephone or online.

Also, unlike the SAT I, you can't cancel a test score for any reason. However, because each test score is released individually, if you retake the exam, you can choose not to report a bad test result.

One other important point: There is no guessing penalty. If you guess and you're wrong, unlike the SATs, you don't lose a fraction of a point. It's to your advantage to make an educated guess if you can eliminate some of the choices. For example, if a section has 35 questions and you answer 30 correctly, it pays to guess at the answers for the other five questions. If you get any of them right, you get full credit, and if you get all five of them wrong, you would still get 30 points for that section.

The following table compares SAT I scores and ACT scores. However, it's important to remember that because the SAT I and ACT tests are very different types of exams, you may do better on one than the other.

ACT Composite Score	SAT Combined Score
36	1600
35	1560 to 1590
34	1510 to 1550
33	1460 to 1500
32	1410 to 1450
31	1360 to 1400
30	1320 to 1350
29	1280 to 1310
28	1240 to 1270
27	1210 to 1230
26	1170 to 1200
25	1130 to 1160
24	1090 to 1120
23	1060 to 1080
22	1020 to 1050
21	980 to 1010
20	940 to 970
19	900 to 930
18	860 to 890
17	810 to 850
16	760 to 800
15	710 to 750
14	660 to 700
13	590 to 650
12	520 to 580
11	500 to 510

Reprinted with permission of The Princeton Review, www.review.com.

Bottom line: Which test you take will depend in large measure on what colleges you decide on. According to The Princeton Review, a student with strong vocabulary skills may do better on the SAT I, while a student with strong grammar and reading skills may find the ACT is the better test for her. Similarly, although limited, the ACT includes some trigonometry questions, while the SAT I math section does not. Depending on your math skills, you may do better on one or the other. Choosing which exam to take will be a combination of your own strengths, coupled with the requirements of the colleges you prefer.

Add to Your College Box

Keep the test scores from every standardized test you take. You will probably want to have a separate box to store all the test-prep information you acquire.

What You Need to Know

- Whether or not you hire a tutor, enroll in a prep course, or study on your own, all students need to prepare for the standardized tests they need to take.
- Whether you take the SAT I or the ACT depends on the schools you choose and your own strengths as a test-taker.
- The SAT I test is the most widely used college entrance exam, but there is considerable controversy surrounding its use.
- The ACT is becoming more widely accepted as a college entrance exam.

Chapter 6

The College Search

Coming Up in This Chapter

- Establishing your criteria for colleges
- Reconciling conflicting preferences in colleges
- Using online services and private advisors to search for colleges
- Making the most of college visits

You probably think you've been getting ready for college forever and maybe that your parents have been making plans for you since the day you were born. But now, that you are about to start high school, it's becoming a little more real. Your classes, extracurricular activities, and interests will help you focus on what's important to you in choosing a college.

If your parents went to college, they probably remember starting their college searches in the spring of their eleventh-grade year at the earliest. That's not so anymore. With the increasing use of early decision college applications, the timing of the search moves back to as early as ninth or tenth grade.

The right college for you is so much more than whatever you find in any classroom. Of course, you want to choose a school that offers a challenging academic program that will make you grow intellectually and prepare you for a career. But ...

- You are also choosing a place to live for four years. What is the right setting for you? Rural, suburban, or urban?

- You are selecting a community that should offer you the opportunity for many different kinds of experiences outside the classroom. What kinds of activities, teams, clubs, and outside opportunities are offered?
- You will be searching for a place that attracts the kinds of students with whom you feel comfortable, yet you want more than a collegiate version of your high school. What is the student body like?

In this chapter I'll talk about how to focus on what you want in a school, how to use the checklist in this chapter to develop and refine a list of characteristics that are important to you in a college—and what to do when some of your choices seem to be contradictory. Finally, I'll walk you through the campus visit: what to look for and how to read between the lines and see behind the beautiful scenery. And I'll talk about why the shoes the students are wearing may influence whether or not you even want to take the campus tour!

There are lots of tools out there to help with the process, including websites where you can key in the characteristics you prefer and you get a list of perfect colleges for you to consider. But of course the acronym GIGO—garbage in, garbage out—is the essential element of this equation. If you don't know what you are looking for, if you haven't prioritized the qualities in a school that you think are most important, then the list loses its value. You can't automate this process. Computer searches and even the advice of others like your parents, friends, guidance counselor, or even a private college advisor can only do so much. In the end, it's up to you to figure out what you want in a school because, after all, it's your life.

Bottom line: Developing a list of colleges that are right for you will take time, thought, and effort on your part. Don't rush the process. It's too important a decision to make quickly.

When to Begin

Should you start visiting college campuses before you even start high school? No, unless you are in the vicinity of a school that has always been of interest to you and have the time. You will change a lot over the next five years. Your preferences and priorities will shift, and your intellectual interests may also change. You may think of yourself as a poet now and then discover the magic and mystery of science as you take more advanced classes in high school. Suddenly, med school seems like an intriguing possibility. The point is that you need your middle school and high school years to get to know yourself better before you begin your college search in earnest.

That said, if you are on vacation and near a college campus, go ahead and visit. Look around and check out the student union. Taking a class during the summer at a university gives you a chance to get to know the campus (with all the caveats about how realistic a view of the school is during the summer session, as discussed in Chapter 4.

But you should start to focus on your college search at least midway through your sophomore year, and certainly no later than the fall of your junior year. You will need that amount of time to refine your checklist of college characteristics, research the possibilities, assess your strengths and weaknesses, visit campuses, and develop your list of schools. The timetable has been moved up from the traditional spring of your junior year because of the increased interest in early decision applications (see Chapter 8). In order to make the decision to submit an early decision application—due generally no later than November 1 or 15—you need to have finished your search by early September of your senior year. To be fair to yourself, you have to allow for enough time to make a considered decision.

In the Beginning

At first glance, you might think that this will be a simple process of going through your checklist and marking those characteristics you want in a school. Then all you have to do is match your preferences to a list of institutions that share those traits, right? No, it's really not that clear-cut. You are sure you want an urban school, nothing but concrete city, but then you visit a school that's picturesque, you spot kids in the quad tossing Frisbees, and you start to rethink where you want to live for the next four years. Similarly, you're sure you're ready to go to the opposite coast, or to either coast if you're in the middle of the country, but then you realize that will limit how many times you come home during the year. Or you are a talented artist and ready to dedicate your life to your craft, but you wonder if that means you should only look at art or design schools.

See, it's not so simple. But using the following checklist will help.

Developing Your College List

Rank the following characteristics from 1 to 5, with 5 as very important:

College Location

_____ Within 25 miles

_____ Within 100 miles

_____ Within 200 miles

_____ More than 200 miles away

Climate

_____ Warm weather year-round

_____ Snow

_____ Changing seasons

Setting

_____ Rural

_____ Suburban

_____ Urban

Size

_____ Enrollment fewer than 750

_____ Enrollment between 750 to 2,000

_____ Enrollment between 2,000 and 4,000

_____ Enrollment between 5,000 and 10,000

_____ Enrollment more than 10,0000

_____ **Academics**

Campus Culture

_____ Greek life

_____ Politically active

_____ Gay tolerance
_____ Conservative/liberal
_____ Strong feminist presence
_____ Competitive sports program
_____ Strong performing arts community
_____ Other

_____ **Co-Ed School**

_____ **Single-Sex School**

_____ **Two-Year College/Community College**

_____ **Specialized School** (art, engineering, music)

_____ **Public vs. Private School**

_____ **Religiously Affiliated College**

_____ **Historically Black College**

_____ **Hispanic-Serving Institution**

List other characteristics that are important to you:

_____

_____

_____

_____

_____

Let's take the questions one by one.

Location, Location, Location

Where do you want to spend most of the next four years? This is the fundamental question to consider when you think about college. The campus is going to be your home, and unlike your family home, you get to decide where that is going to be. Where you live won't be based on your parents' jobs but rather on where *you* prefer to live.

There is something romantic about thinking that you can pick up and move anywhere you choose to go. And this certainly is one option when you choose a college. But the decision to go to college a considerable distance away from your home and family does have certain consequences, and you want to be sure you include them in your considerations.

Keep the following in mind when choosing a school that is more than a four-hour car ride from home:

- The greater the distance, the greater the expense in getting to and from school. Consider that you will probably want to come home at least once, if not twice, a semester (if you factor in long weekends, holidays, and intercession, more if you are on the trimester system). When calculating the cost of college, you will have to factor in not only the cost of travel, which can be considerable, but also the time and hassle involved.

- Will it bother you not to come home for holidays and vacations? Are you prepared to spend holidays on campus or with another family? For example, one student at Dartmouth, Hanover, New Hampshire, spent Thanksgiving with the family of his freshman-year roommate all four years of his college experience. It seemed silly to spend the time and money to fly home to his family in Los Angeles when he would be making the same trip less than two weeks later for Christmas vacation. Sure, it got easier as time went on, but it was especially hard his freshman year not to be home for Thanksgiving and see his family and high school friends. Dartmouth is on the trimester plan so they are usually on Christmas break by December 8.

- The ability for your family to be a part of your college life and visit you on campus may be limited by the distance you go from home. Your parents may or may not be able to come for Parents' Weekend. They may not be able to take you out for dinner during exam week or see you as you play in an important game or take the stage in a dramatic production.

- Factor in the cost of getting your stuff to and from college as well. Will you have to store everything over the summer (the cost of that must be included)? How will you get your clothes, computer, CD player, television, etc., to school in the first place?

☞ With all the other adjustments you will have to make as a freshman, is surviving homesickness going to complicate things?

On the other hand …

☞ You may be comfortable being a considerable distance from your family, and choosing to go to a distant school is not necessarily a comment on how close your family is. You can live in the same house and barely speak, or you can be across the continent and share confidences frequently, staying in touch via telephone and e-mail. You have to figure out what works for you and your family.

☞ You may already be comfortable with traveling long distances by yourself or spending vacations without your family. Your choice may be made easier if you opt for a school that is near extended family. One New York student enrolled at the University of Notre Dame, South Bend, Indiana. Although he couldn't get home for fall break or Thanksgiving, he spent those times with his aunt and uncle who lived in Chicago, about two hours from campus.

☞ You may know that you will miss your family, but that is offset by your excitement about being at the school of your dreams. You may be willing to endure homesickness in return for the college experience you have always wanted.

☞ Money is not a problem, and you're not hassled by traveling over vacations.

☞ You're used to traveling distances to see family. One New York student enrolled at the University of Southern California, Los Angeles. But it didn't seem unusual to either the young woman or her parents. Because the family was originally from England, they frequently spent holidays in airports on the way to and from London to visit grandparents. And the parents didn't feel they could object to their daughter's desire to attend school on the West Coast since they had obviously made the decision to live at considerable distance from their own families.

Do You Prefer Hot, Cold, or Temperate Weather?

It's hard to believe that you would choose a college based on the temperature, but actually it's an important consideration. Maybe climate is not the first consideration on your list, but it is something to keep in mind. One Miami, Florida, native spent four years in Washington, D.C., miserable because she couldn't believe the "freezing weather." Although she liked the school, she was depressed when the temperature dropped below 50 degrees. At the first flake of snow, she took to her bed.

Another student opted for Emory University, Atlanta, Georgia, because he wanted to play golf year-round. In fact, six of the eight schools he applied to were in the South because he wanted not only a good academic program, but also the kind of lifestyle warm weather brings.

On the other hand, avid skiers would probably prefer to look for schools where they can continue their sport. Climate is not a deal-breaker, though. If you find a college that has all the other attributes you're looking for but the weather is not your ideal, you may decide that's where you'll compromise.

Setting: Urban, Rural, or Suburban?

This is a more difficult question. What do you want around your college campus? Are you looking for sweet sounds of nature or the throbbing of the city? Where do you currently live? You may be in for some culture shock if you come from a farm community and settle in for freshman year in Chicago. Conversely, you may find the quiet life a bit unsettling if you come from Los Angeles and enroll in Big Sky Country University. It may be a welcome relief, or it may be too much of a contrast. Consider your own interests and how you use the community in which you live. That can help you decide what kind of setting you will find most comfortable.

One student who came from the Big Apple had always enjoyed backpacking and fishing. It wasn't a surprise when he chose to go to school in New Hampshire.

Urban

Some students can't wait to get to the city. Schools like George Washington University in Washington, D.C., are located smack-dab in the middle of Foggy Bottom, just four blocks from the White House. The school may lack lush, green lawns, but it's got an exciting campus life, because, in fact, the whole city becomes the college campus. That's not to say that there isn't lots going on right on the 10-square-block campus—there most certainly is. But you can also go off-campus and find excitement 24/7.

Of course, some would argue that if you choose a city school, you get all the problems of the city as well. Urban colleges usually aren't in an isolated enclave, and that's one of the attractions for many students. The risk of street crime and violence from people unrelated to the college may be higher, but many urban colleges say, in fact, that they are safer than their suburban or rural counterparts because they know they have to be. They've already beefed up security because of concern about crime. When considering an urban campus, ask to see the crime statistics on campus. The school must keep them and must make them available when asked.

Finally, *urban* is a relative term. You may be in a city, but not necessarily in a big, bustling city. Akron, Ohio, isn't New York City. So while Akron is a fun place to be, you also need to consider what kind of city you want to be in.

Rural

Colleges located in a rural area far from a big city have an appeal all their own. The isolation builds a strong sense of community. The campus can expand and grow as needed, and it's not limited by the surrounding area. You may prefer a quieter, more natural environment that's only available at a rural school, like Oberlin College in Oberlin, Ohio. Of course, the downside is that your entertainment is limited to what is available on campus.

One disadvantage of a more isolated campus is its accessibility. Frequently, train and air travel to the vicinity are limited. You may find that the easiest (even, the only) way to get to the area is by car or bus. Having a car on campus may make it easier for you to get to and from school as well as to any nearby town. If you don't own a car, you'll have to rely on others for rides, which can be a nuisance. If you are concerned that you will eventually feel stifled by a rural environment, remember that most schools offer some off-campus options, such as studying abroad or at other colleges for a semester.

Suburban

Colleges that are located in the suburbs of a city, like Emory University in Atlanta, Georgia, often enjoy the benefits of both urban and rural worlds. Students find they are close enough to participate in the excitement and activities of a city, while still living on a picturesque, self-enclosed campus. There is at least an illusion of greater safety—but check the crime stats and the attention paid to security. Plus, having a car on campus is easier than at an urban school.

Size: Big, Medium, or Small?

Size is a matter of perspective. If you come from a high school with graduating class of 100, a school of 2,000 may seem large. There are colleges where the undergraduate enrollment is under 500 students—that is definitely a small college. But most advisors would suggest that a school would be considered small if it has an undergraduate enrollment of fewer than 2,000. A medium school would include colleges with undergraduate enrollment of 2,000 to 4,000 students. And a large school has more than 5,000 undergraduate students. And then there are the really large schools with undergraduate enrollment of more than 10,000 students.

But it's not as simple as "Do you want to be a big fish in a small pond or a small fish in a big pond?" As Michael Barron, director of admissions at the University of Iowa, Iowa City, points out, you need to know "what systems are in place, what services are available, to suggest that you, the student, are important." The University of Iowa, for example, with 18,000+ undergraduates, has a strong Academic Advisory Center that makes personal, one-on-one connections beginning with incoming freshmen. That helps transform a big school into a smaller community. The University of Michigan, with an undergraduate enrollment of 24,000+ students, becomes a small college if you are admitted to the school's Honors Program. Accepting only 400 to 450 students each year, the Honors Program offers special housing and courses. Some would argue students get the advantages of a large university with the intimacy of a small college.

Large schools usually offer a more diverse student body and, consequently, a wider range of activities. The sports teams may be more competitive—making the collegiate atmosphere more exciting. There may be a wider range of courses available because of a larger faculty. Should you choose to change your major, you may have more options.

But on the other hand, there can be an anonymity on a large campus, and the quieter student might get lost. You will need to find your niche in a large school. It may take time to create your own community within the larger one.

Bottom line: Don't assume that the numbers will either overwhelm you or leave you unfazed. If you have time, visit a large university so you see how a school of 10,000+ actually works. It's hard to imagine it if you don't have this firsthand experience. Talk to other students about how they have created a personalized collegiate experience.

A medium- or small-size school may be able to offer a more personalized program. You may have the opportunity to create your own major and work more closely with your faculty advisor. Smaller campuses seem to have a comfort and support system built in.

But you may get bored and restless when surrounded by the same people for four years. Again, off-campus programs may be a way to enrich the small-school experience, but you still have to spend three years or so at the college.

Bottom line: When you visit small schools, talk to some juniors and seniors. What are their impressions of a small community after two years?

Academics

There is obviously a lot more to college than just the coursework, and in your search you'll need to pay attention to what prospective colleges can offer you academically. You'll also need to think about what you want to study. There are courses and majors offered that you probably haven't even heard of (unless you've been reading college course catalogues for fun), so don't feel like you have to come up with a specific area of study now. Part of the beauty of college is that you have the opportunity to academically explore new areas and interests.

But you do want to be sure that the colleges that interest you offer the programs you want. For example, one student was interested in becoming a teacher. He considered several schools but discovered they didn't offer undergraduate degrees in education. Although there are other ways of becoming certified to be a teacher, he wanted a school where he could complete his teacher education requirements in his four years of college.

Make a list of the majors you think might interest you. Take a look at a college course catalog, either online or in print, of a large school or a college you think you'd like to attend to review the possibilities they offer.

Campus Life

Colleges, no matter what their size, are teeming with extracurricular activities and athletics. You will undoubtedly find new interests you will want to explore once you to get to school, but make of list of the sports and clubs that are important to you now.

- ➭ Do you want a school that has a competitive sports program? Do you envision yourself in the stadium cheering your school team to victory? Do you hope to play for a college team or play intramural sports? List the sports programs you hope your college will have, including sports you've never played before. One student joined the Vassar College, Poughkeepsie, New York, rugby team although he'd never played the sport prior to college. Another high school football player, who was too small to be recruited to play college ball, managed to win a spot on the University of Pennsylvania Sprint Football Team (where players weigh fewer than 150 pounds). He got to indulge his love of the sport while attending a great school.

- Are you interested in writing for the college newspaper? Most schools have newspapers, but if journalism is a possible major for you, check to see if the college paper is published daily. That will make a big difference in the long run because you learn the demands and discipline of publishing a daily paper.

- Are you interested in possibly joining a fraternity or sorority? If so, add Greek life to your list of clubs you hope are on campus. It's also important to note if you prefer that the school not have an active Greek life. The social scene at a college is influenced by how strong the Greek life program is, which is usually indicated by the percentage of students who join fraternities and sororities. You can usually find that information on the college's website or ask about it when you visit the school.

- What other activities would you like to see? It's not just a question of your active participation; you may want to see a strong drama presence on campus, not because you hope to star in the plays, but just because you enjoy going to the theater.

Student Body: Co-Ed, All-Female, or All-Male Colleges?

The demographics of the student body aren't a matter of good or bad, they're just different. Of the more than 3,500 colleges and universities in the United States, more than 98 percent of them are co-ed. There are 78 all-female colleges in the United States (versus 298 in 1960) and only 3 all-male colleges (Morehouse College in Atlanta, Georgia; Wabash in Crawfordsville, Indiana; and Hampden-Sydney in Hampden-Sydney, Virginia). There are about 47 other all-male schools in the United States, but they are primarily seminaries and schools affiliated with religious institutions.

Of course, some all-female schools have close ties to co-ed institutions so that students can have both experiences. For example, Barnard College, New York, is located across the street from co-ed Columbia University. Barnard students may enroll in Columbia courses, and most take more credits on the Columbia campus.

The arguments in favor of single-sex colleges are as follows:

- The level of competition for the opposite sex is reduced. That changes the community atmosphere.

- Gender issues are removed from the equation when deciding leadership positions.

- Especially during the week, the focus is on schoolwork, while weekends are reserved for social occasions.

- Many students who opt for single-sex colleges say the friendships they develop are stronger because they're not hampered by competition for the opposite sex.

The arguments in favor of co-ed colleges are as follows:

- The real world is co-ed. Colleges should mirror that.

- It makes you more comfortable with the opposite sex when you interact with them on a daily basis, not just for social occasions.

- You see the opposite gender as colleagues, not sex objects.

- There is a less of a distinction between the academic world and the social world. Life is not divided into schoolwork and social life but instead is intermingled.

Two-Year Schools (Community College)

Academically, athletically, economically, or emotionally you may prefer a two-year college. Most community colleges have faculty with the same academic credentials as those you will find at four-year institutions, however, the emphasis at two-year schools is on teaching, not research.

Here are some advantages of two-year schools:

- A two-year program permits you to strengthen your academic record. This is especially helpful if your high school record is weak. Some community colleges have open admissions, so if you've earned your high school diploma, you can enroll in classes regardless of your grade point average.

- A two-year school may make sense for athletes who are looking for additional experience and hope to be recruited by a larger institution if they play well at a smaller school (see Chapter 2).

- Economically, two-year schools often are less expensive than four-year colleges. Most community colleges have flexible schedules so you can work and go to school at the same time.

- You may prefer a two-year program, if you want to stay closer to home.

- Most community colleges have smaller classes than four-year public universities. You may prefer—or need—the more personal attention.

Specialized Schools: Engineering, Agricultural, Music, Art, Etc.

You may know exactly what you want to do with your life. You may have known it for years. So a specialized school, where the emphasis is on your subject area, may make sense. John Murray, who teaches AP art at Mamaroneck High School, Mamaroneck, New York, faced a similar dilemma when applying to colleges. He finally had to decide between Rhode Island School of Design, a premier art school, and Yale University. When asked to explain why he chose a liberal arts university over a specialized school, he says, "I learned how to draw in my art classes, but I learned what to draw from my other classes." Art school (or a music conservatory, engineering school, or any other specialized program) may be the right choice for you, but a broader educational experience may add richness to your career.

Public vs. Private School

If you need financial aid, even substantial amounts, in order to attend college, don't assume that a public university is your only option. Although it's true that most public institutions are less expensive than private colleges, particularly for in-state residents, the financial aid packages you receive from a well-endowed private college can put that school within reach. Furthermore, some schools are need-blind, which means they are committed to admitting students without regard to their financial circumstances *and* will put together a financial aid package to make it possible for the student to attend. While this means that the college will not consider if you need financial aid in deciding whether to admit you, it doesn't mean that it will be a free ride. Most financial aid packages include low-cost student loans, so you will probably graduate with college debt. On the other hand, the financial aid packages from public universities are also primarily low-cost loans. (See Chapter 9 for more information on financial aid.)

Religiously Affiliated Colleges

Some religion-based schools have only a historical affiliation with a religious faith. For example, Emory University was founded in 1836 by the Methodist Church but is nondenominational today, and the student body is religiously diverse. On the other hand, College of the Holy Cross, Worcester, Massachusetts, defines itself as "an exclusively undergraduate liberal arts college that embraces a Catholic, Jesuit identity." Faith is a part of the daily life of the college, and the student body is primarily Catholic (although ethnically, economically, and racially diverse).

Attending a faith-based institution can enrich your college experience. It makes it easier to participate in the holidays and rituals of your religion, and you are surrounded by students who share your faith.

However, for reasons of faith, these schools may bar certain courses or student groups, and there may be strict rules for social behavior among students. Diversity may be limited, and the easy, open exchange of ideas may also be restricted or unavailable.

Historically Black and Hispanic-Serving Institutions

There are about 85 schools where the mission is to educate African Americans. There are about 135 institutions designated by the federal government as "Hispanic serving," meaning that at least 25 percent of the student body is Hispanic.

In one of these schools you find a strength and commitment to heritage and a student body who shares those ideals and similar backgrounds. African American students who choose to attend historically black colleges enjoy the opportunity to attend a school where they are in the majority. That is true for most Hispanics who attend Hispanic-serving institutions as well. But lack of diversity in the student body, however, may be a drawback because an important part of the college experience is seeing things from the perspective of different racial and ethnic groups.

The Character of the School

Schools get reputations. Some are known as party schools and the students are lightweights. Others are known to be super-serious and the students are grinds. Frequently, the reputations aren't entirely accurate or, at least, don't do the college justice. But you do have to think about the kind of campus environment you are looking for when you're looking at colleges.

Part of that environment equation is the types of students you hope to see on campus. Diversity is a good thing. Part of going to college is expanding your world and learning from your peers as well as your teachers. But you need to feel comfortable on campus. It's hard to define the character of a school, and the course catalog can't tell you the details, but you want to figure out what you hope the social life on campus will be like, and you need to understand the campus culture. For example, at the University of Georgia, Athens, football games are almost a religious experience: On game day the student body dresses in the red and black school colors, the tailgating parties are elaborate, and school spirit is at its peak. It's not that there aren't plenty of other things to do on campus—hundreds of clubs and activities are available. But the Bulldogs are an integral part of the character and culture of the University of Georgia.

Look for how colleges spend their money. Most schools focus on centers of excellence, areas where they expand and enhance certain programs. It's not an either-or proposition—either you have a football team or a theater program—but it does mean that the college has put its resources into adding faculty or building new facilities to support certain activities. For example, a Big Ten school like Ohio State University has invested millions of dollars in their football program. It is part of who they are. Another school, like Adelphi University, has heavily invested in their performing arts program. Adelphi has plenty of sports teams, but an important part of the campus culture is the many opportunities for students to participate and enjoy the arts.

When you think about the kind of campus culture you hope to find, consider the following:

- How do you like to party? Do you enjoy small, intimate gatherings or toga parties? Are you looking forward to formal occasions, and do you hope that the college will have opportunities for you to dress up? Or would you be happy if you never got out of T-shirts and jeans?

- Are politics important to you? Some campuses are very politically oriented. They have College Democrats and College Republicans, plus a host of other political parties are represented. There are activist campuses, and those schools where it's hard to get out the vote. Political activism can also mean that it's a campus where students fight for causes they believe in. Where do you want to be?

- Are you concerned about gay issues? Schools where a gay student feels more comfortable also attract students who are straight and simply want to be in a more tolerant, liberal atmosphere.

- Are you interested in feminist, black, or Hispanic groups? How diverse is the campus culture? Is there a place for everyone, or are some groups marginalized? How much of a separatist movement is there on campus? Do ethnic and racial groups fully socialize with each other?

- Liberal vs. conservative? Is the campus known to be one or the other? Is that reputation important to you?

- How serious are you about your studies? Some schools are known for being very serious. Students work hard and are under a lot of pressure to achieve. The reputation may not be fully justified, but those schools tend to attract a certain type of student. If you are a really serious student, you may be comfortable in that environment. It doesn't mean that you will never party, but it does mean that you will be surrounded by other students who take their coursework very seriously.

Surfing the Web for Answers and Other Sources of Info

There are several good online sites that will help you begin to develop your list of colleges. Check out the College Board website at www.collegeboard.com, as well as the *U.S. News & World Report* website at www.usnews. com. Each has a search engine that lets you key in certain characteristics and then provides a list of colleges that meet those your criteria.

But don't rely exclusively on computer-generated responses to search for schools. To build your list of colleges, try some of the following:

- College fairs. Some schools, school districts, or associations sponsor college fairs. These bring together a large number of college representatives to talk to prospective students. Visit the various booths, pick up informational brochures, sign up to be on the school's mailing list, and ask the rep questions.

- Word-of-mouth. No matter how much a student raves about or disses their college, you need to listen with a discerning ear. A school that is perfect for one student can be a disaster for another. Similarly, what doesn't work for one student can be a good match for someone else. Take the time to listen. You may hear about programs, activities, and features that pique your interest.

- College counseling centers. Many colleges send members of their admissions departments to high schools to talk to prospective students. Go to a variety of these meetings because they are easy introductions to schools. Be sure to sign in when you go, because admissions officers do keep lists of those students they meet and are on the lookout for those students' applications. Attending these meetings is a sign to a college that your interest in the school is genuine and more than just an easy, computer-generated application.

Contradiction in Terms

Why are you sure that you need to be in a city, where concrete makes up the quad, yet you are intrigued when you hear about Kenyon College, a small liberal arts school in Gambier, Ohio? Sometimes the apparent contradiction is easily resolved. If you love the arts or writing, you would find Kenyon a wonderful school. Actors Paul Newman and Allison Janney are both graduates of Kenyon. So although you won't find the excitement of the Big Apple in Gambier, you will find a thriving theater community.

This is an important thing to remember. Part of what you are doing in your college search is putting your criteria into some type of order. You may want a school with an outstanding football program but also want a small school with fewer than 3,000 students. That eliminates the Big Ten kinds of colleges, but that doesn't mean you can't find a school that has great school spirit and successful Division-III programs.

Furthermore, your preferences aren't always consistent. You can like chocolate and vanilla ice cream—and you can be intrigued by a huge school and a small college at the same time. Just figure out what makes you like both. Something is appealing—what is it?

Don't try and narrow down your list too quickly. Take the time to amass a group of colleges, even if at first glance they appear conflicting. Then take the time to try and figure out what it is they have in common.

Private College Counselors

You may think you need help with this entire college admissions process. Your high school guidance counselor is a good resource, but some students choose to use a private college advisor.

Important: Even if you choose to go the private advisor route, do not ignore or antagonize your high school counselor. You *need* your counselor. He is the one who writes the recommendation that accompanies your applications to college.

The reasons vary for using a private advisor:

- ✏ Your high school counselor is burdened with a heavy student load and can't give you much individual attention.
- ✏ You don't have a relationship with your counselor and don't feel comfortable talking to him or asking for his advice (see Chapter 7 for how to

help your high school counselor write a good letter of recommendation for you, regardless of your relationship).

- You need an extra buffer between you and your parents as you work through the college applications process.

- You have special issues, such as learning disabilities, and need additional help through the search process.

If you decide to use a private advisor, remember:

- *No one* can promise you admission to any college. If someone suggests that he can, find someone else.

- Ask the counselor if he belongs to any professional associations, like the National Association of College Admissions Counseling. If not, ask why. Some advisors don't find the groups helpful.

- Don't let anyone take over the process for you, complete the applications, or write the essays. The advisor should give advice and suggestions, but this is your life. Take control.

- Get a written statement that details the costs and services that will be provided *before* you sign up.

Should you tell your high school counselor that you are working with a private advisor? Probably not. There's not much incentive for the high school counselor to work overtime for a student when he knows a private advisor is also involved.

Should a private advisor write a letter of recommendation for a student? Stephen Bauer, a private college advisor in Larchmont, New York, says he rarely writes a letter of recommendation except when the student has learning disabilities that he thinks need to be explained to a college. On the other hand, Willis Stetson, dean of admissions for the University of Pennsylvania, says that he isn't bothered by private advisors writing on behalf of an applicant if they can add something significant on the student's behalf.

The Campus Tour

Once you have a list of schools that interest you, it's time for a road trip. Visiting the schools is the only way you can make a final decision where you will apply. So let's go.

It's a beautiful day, and the sun is shining brightly. You're decked out in a brand-new State U T-shirt and comfortable shorts, and your running shoes move crisply over the brick walkway that lines the quad. Your tour of the campus starts in 10 minutes, so you've got some time to just look around. Turn your head in any direction, and you're greeted by an array of educational edifices, looming structures with names like "Molecular Biology Center" and "Primate and Reptile Laboratory." As you savor the raw knowledge of the environment around you and soak up the intellectual capacity of the moment, you reach for your bottle of water to take a sip and ...

BAM! All of a sudden your face is covered in H_20 and you're flat on the ground, the result of a hit-and-run from a slovenly sophomore, his dingy tank-top advertising his eternal allegiance to Phi Iota Gamma (PIGS RULE!) and a battered bicycle serving as his getaway vehicle. Whereas three seconds ago you stood in awe of the institution that you hope will not only accept you into its inner sanctum but also teach you how to survive in this crazy world, now you sit on the ground—a quick joke for the Alpha girls that stroll by on their way to lunch.

Hi college, great to meet you.

Okay, so whether or not that story actually happened to anyone we know, there are lessons to be learned. First, visiting a school you think you might want to attend is a must, because even if something as horrific as the preceding tale actually happens (heaven forbid), the experience of physically seeing a school is invaluable. No amount of brochures, pamphlets, or website photos is going to be able to give you any sort of real gauge on what *happens* at a particular school, so it's up to you to find out for yourself. Second, it's important to see the entire picture—not just the buildings or the academics or the rankings of a particular school. Third—and most crucial—keep your head up.

Step One: Planning Ahead

One of the things you'll learn in college is that planning is the key to success. You'll never have time for that late-night party if you don't get your microbiology homework done early, right? Well, along those same lines, if you show up at a college that you're interested in attending but don't have a plan for how you're going to look at it, you'll end up wandering around aimlessly.

So before you even leave your house, make some arrangements. The easiest way is by calling the admissions office of the school you're interested in visiting and telling them that you are coming down on a particular weekend. If you're lucky, they'll just take over and start telling you about information sessions, tours, and class visits. If you're not so lucky, there are some things you'll want to make sure get covered.

If the person on the phone doesn't suggest it, ask about making reservations for your visit. It can pay to have a spot locked up for one of the campus tours, particularly since weekends are the busiest times for tours (because everyone wants to visit on the weekends). If you're going to be arriving at the school on a Friday afternoon, for example, don't assume that the only tour you can take is on Saturday morning. Many schools offer early evening tours, and these can be less crowded (which means that you'll be able to get to know the guide better).

Also, find out if the school has some sort of pre-frosh dormitory visit program. At many schools, freshmen will sign up to be hosts for visiting high school seniors, allowing them to stay in their dorm rooms and taking them out for a few nights. If you don't know a student at the school you're visiting, this can be an easy way to find out more about the people and environment of the college.

Bottom line: Just showing up on campus probably won't tell you much about a school, so get on the phone and make arrangements to see it from all sides.

Step Two: The 411

The first structured activity you'll encounter when you arrive on campus is the *information session*. Most schools offer some type of meeting, which usually consists of a university representative talking to you and your parents in some sort of crowded conference room within the admissions office building. Typically, this is the arena where you'll hear buzzwords like "high graduation rate" or "diversity." Pay attention here, because these people won't lie to you. But you also shouldn't take their words to be gospel, either, because it's highly unlikely that these students are going to tell you anything negative if they're working for the school.

Ask questions about your major, housing, cost of living, the gym, class sizes, or anything else important to you. Don't be afraid to ask any question that seems relevant to you. If you think you want to be a teacher, for example, find out if the school offers a teacher certification course—and if it doesn't, ask what previous teaching candidates at the school did. Of course, you've got to be realistic about the person with whom you're talking. Some representatives will be wholly honest and open with you, but if you sense you're getting a snow job, either ask a follow-up question or make a note to find a student's opinion on the matter.

This is also the time you'll probably acquire some paper—lists of available majors, financial aid fact sheets, important dates and calendars, and all types of other material you may or may not ever actually read. Much of it will be stuff that your parents will be interested in seeing (read: tuition breakdowns), but make sure you keep it. If you actually attend this school, it's likely that the packet you got at the information session will have some relevant documents.

Finally, even if you sleep through the information session itself (this is not advised), make sure you sign in *somewhere*. If the person running the session doesn't have a sign-in sheet, stop at the admissions office front desk before you leave. It's important that the university has a record of your visit.

Why? Well, put it this way: If you were running a club and you had 50,000 people send you the same application for the club but some of the people had come and visited you at your clubhouse, don't you think you'd believe that those people were the ones who *really* wanted to join your club? When it comes down to decision time, particularly if you apply to schools on the common application, admissions officials are going to know whether you visited them or not—and if you did, there probably won't be that question of "Will he come here if we accept him?" That's a good thing.

Bottom line: The information session will give you a general—very general—overview of just about everything at the university. Take it at face value and then investigate more on your own. And make sure you sign in!

Don't Judge a Book by Its Cover

The information session is often the first contact you'll have with someone at the school you're visiting, and although you shouldn't discount your first impression, you shouldn't become attached to it, either.

One student remembers how one of his information sessions began: "The admissions officer came in and said 'How many of you want to be doctors?' and some kids raised their hands. Then she said, 'How many of you want to be lawyers?' and some others raised their hands. Then she asked a few more professions until just about everyone in the room had raised their hand at one point or another. And then she said in a sort of snippy voice, 'Well none of you should come here, because you should be coming here with an open mind.'"

After hearing that little pearl of wisdom, the hero of our story was turned off big time. After all, he was looking for some answers about the school itself, not sarcastic career advice. But instead of going through the rest of his day with a negative view about the university, he tried to meet as many other people as he could. What he found was that very few people had the same attitude as this one woman in admissions, and he really got along with everyone else he met. His questions got answered, and he enjoyed his visit. He learned a valuable lesson: An admissions officer may be a representative of the college but may not represent the scope, depth, and values of the institution very well. You have to find the "truth" through your own efforts.

By the way, he graduated from that very same school four years later.

Bottom line: Don't let a single encounter influence your opinion of a school. Some students are so turned off by the tour guide that they never look at the school. Maybe the individual really is representative of the school—but maybe she isn't. Keep an open mind.

Step Three: These Boots Are Made for Walkin'

College tours with your parents aren't as exciting as touring with the Stones. Instead of groupies, you've got a student admissions representative who walks backward while he talks to you about the library, and instead of sipping champagne backstage after the show, you're sucking down a Sprite with your kid sister. Still, the physical act of walking through the campus you're thinking about living on is a crucial part of your collegiate decision-making process.

When you show up for the tour, it pays to be prepared. Wear comfortable shoes, and take some clothing precautions if it looks like it might be cold or rainy—some campuses have umbrellas for their tour-takers, but plenty don't. These tours can be lengthy, too—if you're traveling with a much younger sibling or a much older grandparent, consider asking in advance how long the tour will take, and if there is a lot of walking up and down hills or stairs.

Silly as it might sound, listen to the tour guide when you're actually on the tour. He won't just be pointing out academic buildings, but will also indicate where students congregate to study or eat. The guides will also filter in information about things that may or may not have been covered in the information session—pointing out where the newspaper or radio station is located, for example.

It's good to ask questions during the tour, particularly if the guide seems amenable to answering. Don't interrupt him when he's explaining something to the whole group, but as you're leaving an area, it's okay to hang back and start a quick conversation with the guide. Again, don't expect him to summarize the university in 10 words or fewer—if you put him on the spot for an answer, recognize that he may not be able to give you a complete one.

In many instances, a guide may gloss over something you're particularly interested in—athletics, perhaps, or the theater scene. Remember that a tour is a limited amount of time, and just because the guide doesn't focus on something doesn't mean it's not an integral part of campus life. If you've got more questions, ask the guide at a convenient moment or write your question down and ask after the tour is over.

Most important, try to take in the physical presence of the place itself. Get a feel for how the students move and walk on campus—you may be able to sense whether the campus is fast- or slow-paced. Do students run from class to class, or walk and talk with each other? Is there green space to sit or lie down and read? Are there benches? There are no "right" answers to these questions, but they ARE important because if you go to this school, you will become one of those students—and you need to be sure you can see yourself in that environment.

Check out the students you see on campus. Do you feel like these are the types of people who could be your friends? One high school junior about to begin a tour of a well-known college, looked around and told her parents, "I can't go here. All the girls wear flats." Her parents were dumbstruck that their daughter was focused on the footwear of the students she saw, but soon they realized that as a strong athlete, usually clad in sneakers, their daughter was really saying that she didn't see other girls who dressed as casually as she did. Obviously, not all the female students on this campus wore dress shoes, but part of your reaction to a college is on a "gut level." Do you feel comfortable here?

Bottom line: The campus tour is not just an opportunity to look at a few buildings. It's a chance to envision yourself within a particular community. While you're on the tour, imagine yourself walking around as a "resident" and see how it feels.

Choose Your Own Adventure

Depending on your mood that day, the campus tour may seem to go by in a flash or it may feel like you're a nomad, wandering endlessly through uncharted terrain. Either way, the likelihood is that you're not going to be able to see everything that is important to you in the time allotted.

So if you've got some time, go back and take a closer look at the things you know will be a part of your daily life if you come to this school. If you're a workout rat, take a few minutes and stop back at the gym to see what sort of weights and machines are available. If you're a radio guy, stop in at the station and say hello to whomever is working that shift, just to make a contact and see how the operation works.

These little side trips can be as valuable as the tour itself, because they're focused on things that you know are important to you. On the other side of the coin, though, don't short-change yourself if you are forced to do a self-guided tour. If you miss all the scheduled tours the admissions office offers, they may give you a detailed map that lays out the campus and points out the stops that the regular tour makes.

Do yourself a favor and hit all the spots if you can. Remember, you want to get the whole picture. Once you've got that, you can focus in on the areas that interest you most.

Step 4: "Bueller? … Bueller? …": Visiting a Class

If you're like most Middle or high school students, the idea of going to an extra class ranks somewhere on the desirability meter below running wind sprints and eating cafeteria food. But when you're considering a school (particularly if it's one you're *really* considering), it pays to check out what the learning environment is like before you enroll.

At some schools, you don't get to choose what kind of class you attend—the admissions office arranges for you to sit in at a particular time, often giving you the name of a student in the class to talk to afterward (and get you back to the admissions office without getting lost). In many cases, though, you can request to attend a class in an area in which you're interested.

When you actually get to the class, try and introduce yourself to the teacher before the class begins, if it's possible. This cuts down any possibility that the prof will look at you and say "Who are you?" during the course of his lecture, thus causing you a certain amount of unnecessary embarrassment. That doesn't happen often, but if you do introduce yourself, you'll be able to approach the prof after the class is over and ask him any questions you might have about the curriculum or subject matter.

During the class, it's not necessarily important whether or not you have any grasp of the material. If you do, great—feel confident that you're already well ahead of some of your high school friends. But if you don't, don't worry about it. You could have walked in to the middle of a discussion that began weeks ago, or you could have landed in a class where a prerequisite course is needed to fully understand this course's material. And don't rule out the possibility that the rest of the people in the room don't have a grasp of what's going on, either.

What is important, however, is to take some notes on the general feeling in the class. Is the class small? Is the classroom large? If you're in a 100-level (beginning) class and there are only 20 students present, you might want to ask if that's a normal class size at the school. Is there much interaction between the students and the professor, or is the professor dominating the dialog? Again, there are no right answers here, but it's information that is important to have.

Bottom line: Attending a class is, as always, a chance to learn. Except in this case, you're trying to learn what taking a class at *this* university is all about. Pay attention to the dynamics and specifics, and then ask questions to find out if what you saw is typical. Keep in mind, one professor won't tell you everything about how classes or run, it will just give you an inkling of the system.

Step Five: House Party (Dorm Visits)

If you've ever seen the classic college movie *P.C.U.*, you know that a pre-frosh dorm visit offers a lot more opportunity than your standard Saturday night in High School–ville. Whether you stay with a friend or a student assigned by the university, this is your opportunity to interact—on more levels than you might imagine—with the student body.

In short, this is your chance to see what *life* as a college student at this particular place is all about. Depending on the type of person that is hosting you, you might do any number of things during your visit—dinner with a bunch of people or dinner with a few; out to a movie or to a political debate; out to a fraternity party or in for a floor party—the possibilities are endless. This is your chance to put the information you heard from the admissions representative to the test. A school may claim to be "right next to the city," for example, but if no students talk about going out downtown, it pays to ask them why they avoid it.

The best piece of advice for this type of situations is to be open to just about everything. Try to rid yourself of the preconceived notions you had of the school before you got there, and if you can't do that, ask your host to either confirm or deny those notions for you. When you're out, don't be judgmental—remember that your host chose to go to this place and you don't want to say anything that will offend him. If your host has extreme feelings—good or bad—about the school, try to get him to talk about the other side of things. If he is always talking about how everything is "the best ever," ask him about the one thing that could be better. And vice versa. If you had questions about your likely major that didn't really get answered at the information session, now is the time to ask your host if he knows anyone in that major—and then ask that person your question.

Again, take note of what the people you see are doing. Whatever it is—drinking, doing drugs, talking, sleeping, dancing—try to find out if it's normal at that school. Try to build an image of what life is typically like at the school, both by watching and asking your host. Most of the time, your host won't have any problem with answering your questions and will often offer lots of additional information.

Perhaps most important, however, is to be careful on these visits. You don't need to impress anyone when you're a pre-frosh, particularly not the people you meet at parties. Whether or not you can drink like a 21-year-old is irrelevant to whether or not you'll be accepted at *any* school. And whatever a frat boy or sorority girl might tell you, in all likelihood, most of the people you meet at a party as a pre-frosh won't remember you if you actually attend the school next year.

So know your limits—and if you don't know your limits, make the ones you use for that night pretty strict. The only way a dorm visit is ever truly horrible is if you end up in the hospital at the end of it.

Bottom line: Dorm visits offer you answers to questions that you won't be able to get at information sessions or tours. Go and have fun—but be careful.

Step Six: Afterward

So it's Sunday night, and you're unpacking your suitcase as you think back on the weekend you just spent at State U. Wow. Pretty campus, interesting classes, great parties—college sure is cool, right? Well, before you start measuring yourself for a cap and gown, take a second and write down your impressions. When May rolls around and you're weighing the pros and cons of several schools, you'll be happy that you've got more than just blurry memories of some professors talking and a couple of trees in the middle of the quad.

Of course, it's also worth mentioning that unless you've got a huge travel budget, you're probably not going to be able to visit every school that interests you. Because that's the case for many students, most schools are willing to mail you videos that give you a quasi-information session from the comfort of your own home. These should be taken with a grain of salt, however, as should any "virtual tour" you might find on a school's website. Remember that these videos are created by the university, not an objective observer, so there probably won't be too much mention of the school's problem with roaches in the locker rooms, for example. These are things that you need to find out on your own, and the best way to do that is by using your own two eyes.

Bottom line: You wouldn't buy a house without looking at it first, so if it's at all possible, avoid making a final decision on a college without making a campus visit.

Narrowing Down Your College List

Once you have a list of the schools that intrigue you, it's time to figure out if your academic record makes you a competitive applicant. Don't look just for easy shoe-ins, but remember to be realistic. Unless you bring something unusual to the table, don't expect to get into Harvard with an 82 average. Compare your academic record to the academic profile of the school.

You can search college websites, the search engines at www.collegeboard.com and www.usnews.com mentioned in earlier in this chapter, and various books (see Appendix A for college directories) for the academic profiles of schools.

Develop a list of 10 to 15 schools that interest you. This isn't the time to try to figure out whether you want to submit an early decision application to any of these schools. (See Chapter 8 for a complete discussion of the early decision issue.) Right now, you just need to find a list of colleges you like. Refine your list of 10 to 15 down to 8: 2 "reaches," 3 "looks goods," and 3 "safeties":

- **Reaches.** These are schools that you love, but that your record may not be strong enough to secure admission to. There are no guarantees on this list. In horse-racing terms, these are long shots, but not out of the realm of possibility. If your academic record is slightly lower than the college profile, the other parts of your application—essay, test scores, recommendations, and extracurricular activities—need to make up for the difference.

- **Looks good.** These are schools you also love, and when you compare your record to the college profiles, you think, "I'm certainly a competitive applicant." But keep in mind that you will have to provide the admissions committees of these schools with reasons to distinguish you from other applicants. You're a good candidate, but so are many other students. You will need to make your case in your application as to why they should accept you. See Chapters 7 and 8 for exactly how to do that.

- ✏ **Safeties.** These are the colleges where you are positive that you will be admitted. Your academic record and extracurricular activities exceed the college profiles. Your safeties list should probably include one of the colleges in your state university system. But here's the most important point about safety schools: You should really like them. They must be colleges you could attend and find the courses you want, the activities you like, and the kind of student body that makes you comfortable. Never choose a safety school you couldn't, if necessary, attend.

Given the quirky nature of college admissions, as well as the nature of financial aid packages (see Chapter 9), you need the flexibility and comfort level of saying, "Any of my eight schools would be fine." That's not to suggest that you don't have a preference, but that if push comes to shove, you could enroll in any one of the eight colleges on your list.

Bottom line: Only choose schools that you like. Realistically, you could end up at any one of them.

Add to Your College Box

Keep your list of college preferences as well as any web searches in your College Box. Also add in the contract if you choose to use a private advisor. You may need to add a second College Box as you add in all the material you will accumulate from college visits and mailings. Be sure to include your impressions of each school you visit, plus the names and addresses of any students you meet during those visits.

What You Need to Know

- ✏ You need to take the time to develop a list of qualities you want in a college and then begin your search for schools that possess those qualities.

☞ The characteristics you seek may seem to conflict, but you need to determine what are the common characteristics among the schools that you choose.

☞ College visits are a valuable way of getting to know a school—something you can't get just from reading about it. Virtual tours and videos are helpful, but they can't capture the flavor of a live campus.

☞ Apply to at least eight colleges, but make sure you could be comfortable at any of the schools to which you are admitted.

Chapter 7

Applications: Part One: The Write Stuff

Coming Up in This Chapter

- College essays give schools a more complete picture of you, your values, and why you want to go to a particular institution

- Carefully selecting a topic, organizing your thoughts, and writing creatively and persuasively are the keys to a successful college essay

- Help teachers and your guidance counselor write clear, positive letters of recommendation for you by providing them with the information they need

The college application process is a lot of paperwork, although in this day of online applications, that's speaking figuratively, not literally. But in any case, there's a great deal of required writing. There's writing that you will be responsible for—most colleges, public and private, require at least one essay as part of your application—and then there's writing that others will do on your behalf—teacher recommendations and your counselor's evaluation. Even though you will not be writing this latter material, it's up to you to provide the information and key points that you hope those who are working on your behalf will use. In this chapter, I'll cover all the "write stuff" you'll need.

The College Essays

Essays and short-answer questions give colleges critical information they can't get by looking at numbers or activity lists. What you write ...

- ✐ Tells schools that you can articulate and defend a point of view.

- ✐ Provides insight into your values. It shows what's important to you and what interests you.

- ✐ Reveals how you think. Are you logical, funny, intuitive, creative, or insightful?

No matter what your major may be, you need to be able to write logically and thoughtfully. To defend your hypotheses in biology, you still must be able to present a cogent argument. So don't think that just because you're not planning to major in history or English, you don't have to be strong writer. College courses are writing-intensive. Being able to write well is central not only to success in college, but to whatever career you choose.

Sarah Myers McGinty, author of *The College Application Essay*, studied the role essays play in the college admissions process. Reporting in *The Chronicle of Higher Education*, McGinty found that the majority of admissions officers at public, private, large, small, highly selective, and less selective schools all rate essays as "somewhat important." However, she adds, "In an individual case, however, the essay can be crucial. A student's essay may not figure prominently in her application to College B, where her numbers are impressive. But at College A—a more ambitious choice—her essay may set her apart from other applicants and get her in."

The Questions

There are three basic college essay questions. Some institutions ask only a single question, while others require several essays plus some shorter responses (four lines or so). And each school has their own way of asking, so you need to see what the purpose of the question is so you can give an appropriate response. Colleges should be able to tell from your answer that you carefully read their instructions and are giving them the information they are seeking. To do so clearly and creatively is the challenge.

✏ Some college essays are designed to learn about you and your values. Some schools ask straightforward questions. For example, George Mason University in Fairfax, Virginia, asks ...

> The Admissions Committee is interested in learning more about you. On a separate sheet of paper, please write at least 150 words about yourself. Please use this essay to relay information about yourself that cannot be found elsewhere on your application. You may choose to write about your future ambitions and goals, a special talent or unusual interest that sets you apart from your peers, or a significant event or relationship that has influenced you during your life.

And the University of Michigan application requires students to ...

> Submit an essay that will help us learn more about you and what you hope to accomplish through a college education. You may emphasize, for example, an important milestone in your life, an educational goal, or an interesting question you have creatively addressed.

Other schools phrase the question more creatively. The application from the University of Virginia, Charlottesville, asks ...

> "The past is never dead. It's not even past." So says the lawyer Gavin Stevens in Faulkner's *Requiem for a Nun*. To borrow Stevens' words, what small event from your personal history or the history of the world, is neither "dead" nor "past"?

The classic essay question from the University of Pennsylvania is: "You have just completed your 300-page autobiography. Please submit page 217."

However they are phrased, these types of questions are focused on you and are designed to give the college an insight into who you are. But in the case of the University of Pennsylvania's question, clearly the question is not only a challenge of who you are, but who you hope to be. If you were filling out this application, you would need to convey how attending the University of Pennsylvania will help you to achieve your goal.

A variation on this question pushes you to examine your values. The University of Virginia requires students to answer the question: "What work of art, music, science, mathematics, or literature has surprised, unsettled, or challenged you and in what way?" Or as one of the university's optional questions asks: "What is your favorite word and why?"

➥ The second type of question asks you to explain exactly why you want to attend a specific school. For example, the application from Swarthmore College in Pennsylvania, goes straight to the point: "Please tell us briefly why you have decided to apply to Swarthmore."

Some ask you to be more specific, requiring you to really know the institution. For example, the University of Pennsylvania requires students to "Describe the courses of study and the unique characteristics of the University of Pennsylvania that most interest you. Why do these interests make you a good match for Penn?" And the applicant must use no more than one page to answer this question. You can't fudge this. You have to do your homework and study the catalog.

➥ Finally, there are the questions that ask you to expand on information you've already provided. For example, Swarthmore's application asks: "Please write a few paragraphs about one or two activities or intellectual or personal interests to which you feel particularly committed." You've already listed all your extracurricular activities on the application, but now you are being asked to explain in detail why you have chosen to devote your spare time to these clubs, volunteer service, etc.

You will need to take time to answer each of these questions, even the short-answer ones, thoughtfully but concisely. McGinty found that admissions officers judge application essays with these criteria:

➥ Correctness

➥ Organization

➥ Specific evidence

➥ An individual style

In the following sections, I'll tell you what you need to do to write the kind of essay that best makes your case.

Plan Ahead

You may work well under pressure, but frankly, this is not the time to test that theory. You need to be thinking about essay topics even before you decide on colleges. Some high schools have you write these types of essays your junior year as practice for the college application process. But in any case, think about your responses to the issues being asked by these kinds of questions.

Topic Troubles

Finding a good topic, especially for those open-ended questions, is one of the toughest parts of the college application. For many students, the problem is that nothing interesting has happened to them in their lives—at least from their perspective. It may be the one time that you wish for some trauma in your life because at least then you'd have an essay topic. But before you go wishing for a tornado to strike your house, rest assured, that is not what the college admissions officer requires.

Yes, colleges do respect students who have overcome adversity. And if you have experienced some type of trauma, and feel comfortable writing about it, consider doing so. But admissions officers are not looking for disease-of-the-week essays. They understand that most 17-year-old applicants have led fairly mundane lives. But that doesn't mean that you have nothing to write about.

For example, one straight-A student wrote the following on his college application to Yale: "I don't fail many tests, but the one I did really hurt. I flunked my driver's test three times." He then went on to describe the humiliation of failing when all his friends sailed right through the test. But the meat of the essay was his explanation of what he had learned from the experience. Failure had taught him resilience and humility, and he had learned to ask for help when he needed it, not seeing it as a sign of weakness. This is the personal growth that colleges want to see.

As Yale University writes in its essay instructions: "Write what matters to you and you are bound to convey a strong sense of who you are." Write about your passions. For example, suppose you love animals and work in

163

the greyhound rescue movement. A description of a specific incident in which you participated gives the admissions officer a much stronger insight into who you are and the commitment you are willing to make to promote something you believe in.

Answer the Question

Be specific. While you will probably be able to use variations of your essay on more than one college application, you need to be sure that it doesn't look like you just cut and pasted it, ignoring what was asked. Tweak your answer so that it is clear you are specifically responding to the college's question.

Especially for questions about why you want to attend a specific college, be careful, very careful. Sure, there are some generic reasons—"College X is known to have a strong history department, and I think I want to major in history"—but you make your case so much stronger when you take the time to look at the course catalog and explain the types of courses, found at College X, that make the institution so attractive to you. For example, "I'm interested in medieval English history, and College X has a strong concentration in that area."

Your Voice Must Emerge

Although it's important to have someone else proofread your essay to correct punctuation, spelling, and grammar, *it's even more vital that the essay remain in your voice.* A parent, guidance counselor, English teacher, or whoever you ask to review your essay can offer suggestions for changes, but you must be the writer. You can discuss topics with an advisor, but the essay must be your words and your thoughts. Not only is this the ethical path, but it's also practical. Admissions officers see hundreds of essays, and they can tell what is from a student and what is manufactured by a professional. They can sense authenticity in a piece, and that's what they want.

Details, Details

Descriptive words make any piece of writing come alive. Let your reader, the college admissions officer, be on the scene with you. If you are writing about your volunteer work in an animal shelter, describe the scents and sounds you encounter there—and how you feel when you walk through the door.

Sports: Avoid the Trite

It's not that you can't write about sports. If sports are your passion, it makes sense for you to make that the focus of your essay. But no college admissions officer wants to hear about how you caught the touchdown that won the game. Congratulations, but where's the personal growth in that? But tell the reader about the contributions you made as the water boy for the team and you'd have a more interesting essay. One student wrote about how being a goalie on his soccer team gave him a perspective on life—seeing the whole game come together from a distance, watching the action, and then narrowing down to the play in front of him and his role. Sports became a metaphor for life—not just a series of kicks and saves.

Make Yourself Human

College admissions officers want to see the real you, flaws and all. The important point is to make sure the reader can see that you face your concerns and deal with them. Again, it's the theme of personal growth.

Be Positive

Even if you are describing some adversity you have met and overcome, you need to put it in the context of the positive aspects of the experience. Focusing only on the negative is a turn-off and is counterproductive. Tell the admissions officer what you have learned about yourself. Did you surprise yourself with your own resilience? Did someone else help you find the courage you needed to deal with a difficult situation?

Short but Sweet

Schools have to review thousands of applications in a short period of time. So if a college gives you a word count or space limitation, they mean it.

They are looking for you to make your point in a concise, meaningful way. It's not always easy, but to have the maximum impact, you need to follow instructions.

Don't Second-Guess the College

Don't try and figure out what the college wants to hear. Write what you have to say. *Don't* deliberately write a provocative statement just to challenge the reader, but *do* make sure that your point of view is clear.

That's Funny?

Humor works, but you have to be careful. As we all know, what's funny to you can bore someone else to tears or even be offensive to someone. It's better to write about a topic in a serious, respectful tone, and submit your contribution to the school's humor magazine as a supplement to your application.

Check Your Facts

This may seem elementary, but make sure you use the correct titles and author names for any literary references you make in your essay. If you are making a historical mention, double-check that you've got the right time and place. In other words, assume your reader is literate and smart. If you make an easily found mistake, it will look like you didn't take the exercise seriously and may suggest that you are not really interested in the school. This is certainly not the impression you hope to give.

Spelling and Grammar Count

It's not enough to run spell and grammar checks although you certainly should. The spelling function on your machine won't pick up homonyms like their, they're, and there. And grammar checks don't always point out punctuation errors. So read and reread your essay. And then find someone else to proofread it again.

Computer Smarts

Whether you apply online or download the application, you need to word process your essays (your entire application, actually). As Rory Shaffer, director of admissions for Adelphi University, points out: Because almost all students can use computers to complete their applications, "there's no excuse for white-out or crossed out words on an application. Make the correction and reprint the page." It's easier on the reader to see a clean, error-free, essay. Typing or printing neatly just isn't as acceptable. If need be, ask to use your school's or public library's computers.

Use a readable font, like a 12-point Times Roman or Arial. Don't use a smaller font size to squeeze in more words. Remember, you want to make your essay easy on the eyes.

Rewrite and Revise

You may be able to write your entire essay in a single sitting—but then you need to put it aside. (Remember the first tip is to plan ahead so you have time to let the essay "sit.") Virtually every written piece benefits from revision and tweaking—strengthening a verb, adding descriptive phrases, or tightening a line of argument.

Bottom line: Take the essay process seriously, because colleges most certainly do. There are no right or wrong answers to the questions posed by these essays. Rather, what you are trying to do is give the admissions officer insight into who you are. By the end of your essay, the officer should feel that they know you better, like who you are, and believe that you will be a valuable member of the college's community.

The Basics of Writing an Essay

The basics of writing an essay haven't changed since you wrote your first composition in elementary school. Let's review:

- **Pick a topic that is self-contained.** You need a small, personal issue that you can address in fewer than 500 words (about one sheet of paper). You can't really address topics such as world peace in this kind of space, and that's not what colleges want to see, anyway.

- **Organize and outline your thoughts.** Before you put pen to paper—or more likely, fingers to keyboard—think about what you want to write about. Then outline the points you want to cover.

- **Start off strong.** Your opening sentence sets the tone for the essay. Grab your reader immediately so he's interested in what you have written. The first paragraph should outline what the point of the essay will be.

- **Use clear, concise, language.** Choose your words carefully. Don't settle for wishy-washy verbs and adjectives, and avoid clichés. You've got the time to play with the vocabulary you use. Make the most of it.

- **Illustrate your points.** Use literary, historical, or even pop culture references if appropriate—but of course, make sure you use them correctly. References are to reinforce your own personal values. Name-dropping is not effective. And of course, make sure you spell the names correctly.

- **Write a dynamite ending.** You need to summarize your points without repeating them. Don't leave your reader hanging. Make it clear what the point of the essay has been, and leave with a final thought.

- **Set it aside for a day.** Build in enough time in your schedule that you can let the essay sit for a day, then read it again with fresh eyes. You may find it helpful to read the essay aloud. That's when you'll notice if you've used the same adjective or verb more than once in a paragraph. You'll see where you can strengthen a phrase or add pizzazz to a point you are making.

Bottom line: Bring every bit of organization and creativity you have to the essay portion of the application. Take care but also take risks. This is an opportunity for you to leave the admissions staffer with a vivid impression, not simply another predictable, fuzzy, "write by the numbers" essay that could have been done by anybody. You want him to think that you would be a great addition to the student body of his college.

What Other People Say About You

Almost all colleges require at least one teacher recommendation, and some ask for two. In addition, colleges also require an evaluation from your high school counselor. Dartmouth College in Hanover, New Hampshire, wants not only two teacher recommendations and one from your counselor, but also a letter of recommendation from one of your peers. No matter how many references a school demands, the point is always for the school to get to know you better.

Teacher Recommendations

Teacher recommendations give the colleges the best insight into your performance as a student. The details required vary from school to school. The teacher recommendation form from the University of Delaware, Newark, is fairly open-ended. It asks: "We are interested in your evaluation of this candidate who is applying for admission to the University of Delaware. In addition to your assessment of the candidate's strengths and weaknesses, we would like to know what makes this student unique or distinctive and what you see as the student's special talents."

In contrast, Stanford University, in California, has a two-page teacher recommendation form that has two checklists to be completed (although teachers have the option of omitting the checklists if they don't feel comfortable with a rating system). It's interesting to see what this top school is interested in learning about you.

The first checklist is about more than your academic abilities. Teachers are asked to rank the student as Below Average, Average, Good, Very Good (Top 10 percent), and Outstanding (Top 5 percent) in the following categories: Initiative/Motivation; Intellectual Curiosity, Oral Communication, Written Communication, Creativity, Energy, Self-Confidence, Leadership/Influence, Responsibility, Integrity, Concern for Others, Respect for Differences, Warmth of Personality, Sense of Humor, Emotional Maturity, Reaction to Setbacks, Respect Accorded by Faculty, and Respect Accorded by Peers.

The teacher is also asked to respond to two specific questions. First is a question on your academic and intellectual abilities. The form asks: "Other parts of the student's application provide details on academic accomplishments. In what ways might you distinguish this student's academic performance from that of other able students? Please comment on the student's intellectual attitude, curiosity and enthusiasm for learning."

The second question is more personal: "What do you like the best about this student? In what ways has the student made an impact in your class, the school or the community? Are there any factors that might interfere with the candidate's academic performance and/or personal relationships at Stanford?"

A final question on the Stanford application is open-ended: "Is there anything else we should know about this student (for example, personal circumstances, unusual accomplishments, obstacles overcome)?"

On the final checklist, the teacher is asked how many years she has been teaching and then asked to "summarize this applicant's promise as compared to that of other-college bound students in your school." There are three categories: Academic, Personal, and Overall, and the following rankings: Below Average, Average, Good, Very Good (Top 10 percent), Outstanding (Top 5 percent), and One of Top Few of My Career. Landing a "one of the top few of my career" ranking from a teacher you respect would be outstanding!

Given these types of questions, you can see why it's so important that you pick the right teacher—someone who knows you well enough to give the details that are required. And you can also see why it's so critical that you provide your teacher with a list of extracurricular activities and community service projects you have worked on. Even if this is a favorite teacher who has known you for years, she is probably writing many recommendations and can use the help keeping all the information straight for each student.

Here's what you need to do to get the best teacher recommendation possible:

- ✒ **Choose carefully which teacher you are going to ask to write a recommendation for you.** Obviously you want someone in whose class you have done well. But equally important, quite simply, you want to choose someone who likes you. Even if you got an A in a class, if it was clear that you irritated the teacher (for whatever reason), find someone else to write your recommendation.

If you are not sure which teacher to ask, talk to your guidance counselor. She may have some insight, gleaned from informal conversations with the faculty, on which teacher is the right one to approach. Also some schools require students to ask two teachers a year to give written evaluations of their work. This helps the counselors guide students to teachers who have given them good recommendations in the past. But it also helps counselors see which teachers, quite frankly, write well—critical information in producing a helpful recommendation for you.

Choose an academic teacher whose class you have had in the last two years. Colleges want to see recommendations from teachers who can write about your ability to handle challenging subjects. If an institution requires more than one recommendation, try and get one from the humanities and one from the sciences/mathematics, assuming you have done well in both areas. This gives the school an opportunity to see your range. But it's better to ask teachers who think well of you, even if they are from the same discipline.

- **Ask the teacher if she can write a strong letter of recommendation for you.** Teachers understand the importance of college recommendations, and most will be honest with you. While it may hurt if a teacher turns you down, it's far preferable to know the truth than risk a less-than-positive reference. If you have done well in her class, ask *politely* why she doesn't think she can endorse your candidacy. That can help you figure out who a better choice would be. Her criticism may not be valid for another teacher.

- **Ask the teacher to write your college recommendation at the beginning of the school year, even before you've narrowed your list of colleges.** Good teachers are asked by many students to write college recommendations, and the process is time-consuming. One English teacher turned down a favorite student because it was late October before he asked and she was already swamped with forms from others. Lorna Minor, an AP American history teacher at Mamaroneck High School in Mamaroneck, New York, says she writes an average of 20 to 30 recommendations each year (from a class of 275 seniors). She estimates that it takes her between one to two hours for each recommendation. (Teachers will generally write one letter of reference and then copy and attach it to each school's form. They don't write separate recommendations for each college, but they may need to spend additional time filling out the other information required by individual institutions.)

Make an appointment to see the teacher to make your request. You want to spend a few moments with him. This isn't a subject that should be approached while passing in the hall between classes. Minor advises her students, generally juniors, to speak to her early in September of their senior year if they would like her to write a letter of recommendation for them.

➥ **Your grade in the class doesn't have to be a deal-breaker.** Even if you have less than a 90 average, especially in an honors or AP class, you can still approach the teacher for a recommendation. As Minor explains, "Colleges are interested in more than just the grade. They want to know from the teacher if the student worked hard, was conscientious, had a good work ethic, participated in class, completed assignments, and had a good attendance record." There are plenty positives to write about if you have been a hard-working student, even if your grade isn't as high as you would have liked.

➥ **You'll be asked to waive your right to read the recommendation.** The Family Education Rights and Privacy Act of 1974 provides that applicants who subsequently enroll in an institution have the right to review the evaluation, unless that waive that right to access. But schools want teachers to feel free to write an honest evaluation without fear of a student coming back with complaints or lawsuits at some later date if he doesn't get in to the school. Your teacher may or may not be willing to share her letter of reference—most do not and will send the letter directly to the college. But if you have chosen wisely, you should feel comfortable that the teacher has your best interests at heart and will write a positive recommendation that will support your case.

➥ **Provide the teacher with a list of your activities and awards. Include the best paper you wrote for his class.** You are trying to make this as easy as possible for the teacher by giving him all the information he will need to write a comprehensive evaluation of you as both a student and a person. Take the time to talk with the teacher so he understands your goals and interests.

✏ **Make it easy for the teacher.** Give the teacher plenty of time to complete the recommendation. Don't give your information to her a week before the letter is due. Provide the teacher with a stamped, correctly addressed envelope for each college form she is completing for you. *Politely* follow up a few weeks later to make sure that she has completed the forms and doesn't need anything else from you.

✏ **Thank you.** Once she has completed the recommendations, be sure and send the teacher a thank you note. Later on, let her know what happens. Thank her again and tell her where you were accepted—and where you have decided to go.

Bottom line: Carefully choose the teachers you will ask to write college recommendations for you. They will give the colleges an important perspective on you. Make their job as easy as possible by providing them with the information they need to paint a complete portrait of you.

Counselor Evaluation

Colleges also ask for a secondary school report, as well as mid-year evaluations (an update on your mid-year grades). Your guidance counselor (or in some cases, principal or headmaster) will complete these forms. The evaluations, like teacher recommendations, can be fairly straightforward. In addition to your GPA, class rank, and tests scores, the University of Delaware asks the counselor to check whether he "Recommends, Recommends with qualifications, Prefers not to make a recommendation, or Not recommends" the student for admission.

Stanford University has a more detailed report to be completed, asking questions similar to its teacher recommendation form discussed earlier. But one question on the counselor evaluation form is especially interesting: "What adjectives immediately come to mind in describing this student."

Here's how you can help your counselor write a positive, detailed portrait of you. Give him a list of your activities, both in school and outside of school, including any honors you have received, as well as factors he should remember when describing you. Provide him with the adjectives you would like to see him use when filling out college forms.

If your mid-year grades are especially noteworthy, ask your guidance counselor to attach a note to the college form that points out how well you are doing in challenging, senior year courses.

Optional Letters of Recommendation

Colleges are inundated with paperwork. When you consider that each applicant's file has a minimum of 7 to 10 forms and that many schools have thousands of applicants—well, that's a lot of papers to shuffle. So you have to be careful about overloading your file.

It's reasonable to ask for an additional letter of reference, especially from a source outside of school—*but only if the person writing the letter has something different to add to your file.* You don't need someone else saying you are a good student—presuming that you have had at least one or two teachers point that out in their own recommendations.

Here's how an additional letter of recommendation makes sense. One student wrote in her college essay about her work with her church's food pantry, what she had learned from the experience, and how it had impacted her future goals. During her college interview, she discussed with the admissions officer her interest in becoming a minister. So it made sense that she included in her college file a letter from her minister telling the school what an exceptional young woman she was and emphasizing her maturity and empathy. This letter added another dimension to the file and reinforced what she wrote about in her essay.

On the other hand, you don't want to look like you're overselling the product (you). If you make too strong a case, with too many extra letters, it can look like your basic record is weak and you need all the help you can get. College admissions officers are not impressed with vague letters from important alumni, political figures, or celebrities. These notes say more about your parents' contacts than your qualities.

So if you are going to have additional references sent to a college, make sure the person writing the recommendation really knows you well. Unless the letter is clearly from someone who is very familiar with you, these letters can have a negative effect. It's more important that the individual who writes your letter have something important to add than who the individual may be. In this case, what is said is more valuable than any name-dropping.

Add to Your College Box

Keep a checklist of who you asked to write letters of recommendation for you, as well as copies of thank you notes sent. Mark down when you follow up with a teacher, and note the date if he tells you when the letter of recommendation was sent.

What You Need to Know

- Plan ahead so you have time to find a good college essay topic, organize your thoughts, write, and then proofread your essay.

- Ask teachers early in the school year if they feel comfortable writing a letter of recommendation for you.

- Give teachers the information on your activities, honors, and future plans so your letters of recommendation paint a vivid portrait of you.

- Additional letters of recommendation can be helpful if they add significantly to your college application by providing specific information about your personality or life.

Chapter 8

Applications: Part Two: What Else You Need to Know

Coming Up in This Chapter

- Students are increasingly using early decision as a strategy for improving their odds of acceptance—but is it right for you?

- Did your parents graduate from a college you're interested in attending? How does being a legacy affect college admissions decisions?

- Some colleges love 'em; others couldn't care less: what you need to know about interviews and how they affect your chances for admission

- The Common Application, supplementary materials, affirmative action, and application do's and don'ts—the final details of applying to college

You have developed your list of colleges. You may prefer one more than the others, but you have made peace with yourself: You could attend any of the eight schools on your list. (Of course, the best-case scenario is that you get into your first-choice college.)

You've written your personal essays, responded thoughtfully to the short-answer questions, figured out which teachers to ask for recommendations, but there are still several issues to resolve before your applications are complete.

Early Decision Dilemma

In the fall of 2001, Duke University received 1,590 applications from students seeking early decision admission, up 22 percent from 2000. Yale's ED applications that same year were up 17 percent. Many other colleges also report record numbers of students who sought an answer to their college quest by mid-December of their senior year. Many of the most competitive colleges are filling up to half of their classes from their early decision applicant pool. And while Yale president Richard Levin has sharply criticized the rising pressure on students to apply early decision to colleges, it doesn't look like the trend is likely to stop in the near future. University of Pennsylvania dean of admissions Willis Stetson counters that Penn is pleased with the applicant pool that applies early and that in recent years the college has admitted between 45 to 50 percent of the incoming class early decision. He doesn't see a need to change the policy he believes benefits both students and the university.

How does this affect you? First, let's define the terms.

Early decision   The student applies to a college with the understanding that if she is admitted, she will attend. Usually, the application deadline is either November 1 or 15. Colleges agree to notify applicants of their decision to admit, defer, or reject by mid-December at the latest. This gives students enough time, should they be deferred or rejected, to apply to other colleges. Some institutions have a second (or even third) cycle of early decision applications with early January or February deadlines and responses within six weeks. (See the later "The Second Cycle of Early Decision" section for information on applying in a second ED cycle.)

Early action   Similar to early decision, but with one critical difference: It's not binding on the student. If admitted, the student still has the option of applying to other schools. Among the Ivy League schools, only

Harvard offers an early action program. The remaining Ivies—Brown, Columbia, Cornell, Dartmouth, Princeton, University of Pennsylvania, and Yale—now offer only a single early decision option. Georgetown University, Boston College, University of Chicago, Massachusetts Institute of Technology, and University of Notre Dame, among others, offer an early action option.

Regular decision   The student applies to colleges by the deadline (which varies from school to school). For many private colleges, the application deadline is January 1 for regular decision, but may be later at some schools. Colleges respond sometime in late March or early April. The student can then choose among the colleges that have offered him admission.

Rolling admissions   Admissions decisions are made as the applications are read, and this continues until the class is filled. Decisions are generally made within six weeks of when the application is filed. However, some public universities choose to place out-of-state applicants in a decision pool for the spring. Because rolling admissions is most common among large state universities, send in those applications early because the schools often fill their housing and main campus fast.

Accept   You're in! Congratulations!

Reject   Sorry, you've been denied admission. Your file is closed.

Deferred   The college is unwilling to accept you as an early decision or early action candidate but will consider your application along with the others in the regular decision pool.

What's in It for the Colleges?

Originally, early decision was for a select few students who knew, without question, what college they wanted to attend. It became a more popular option about 10 years ago, but it has snowballed into an application phenomenon in the last five years among private, elite colleges. Critics would claim this has everything to do with the economics of college admissions and little to do with student needs.

How does a college benefit from a large early decision pool? A 2000 study by the John F. Kennedy School of Government of Harvard

University, titled "What Worms for the Early Bird: Early Admissions at Elite Colleges," lists five important incentives for colleges:

- **Identifying enthusiasts.** Because early decision is a binding process (that is, if admitted, you will come), the college has filled a significant portion of its class with students who want to be there. As Judith Rodin, president of the University of Pennsylvania, points out, "It's terrific to have students on campus who really want to be on campus. That changes the feeling of the place."

  But critics argue that some students have opted to apply early decision as a strategic move. Their reasoning is: "I can get in to that school, even though I really want to go somewhere else. *But* I don't want to waste an early decision advantage."

- **Reducing uncertainty.** By accepting a large number of students early decision, the college can better manage enrollment. There is less uncertainty about final class size and composition.

- **Minimizing financial aid commitments.** This is controversial, but ED critics suggest that early decision applicants are at a distinct disadvantage in applying for financial aid because they can't compare packages from different colleges. Schools often will counter with a better aid package when an admitted student can show the offer from another school (see Chapter 9).

  But it's a different story for colleges, economically. The Kennedy School study confirms that ED applications tend to come from a wealthier group of students who are not asking for financial aid. In large measure, colleges are admitting enthusiastic, full-paying customers. This helps their bottom line and permits institutions to stretch their financial aid funds further.

- **Improving selectivity ratings.** There are a variety of groups that rank colleges, but certainly among the best known and most widely used is the one issued by *U.S. News & World Report* magazine. Whether or not these rankings are valid—and there are certainly significant flaws in their methodology—colleges want to be as high in the rankings as possible. The admissions office can influence two factors of the rankings: selectivity and yield.

Selectivity measures the proportion of how many applicants are admitted, that is, how many students are accepted out of how many applied. Colleges want a low selectivity index. For example, according to *U.S. News & World Report*, Harvard accepts only 11 percent of all its applicants (that includes both early action and regular decision applicants). Actually, the most competitive schools are Julliard, a prestigious music college in New York, which admits only 8 percent of its applicants, and the U.S. Coast Guard Academy, which admits only 9 percent. Harvard is third on the list of most competitive colleges.

Keep in mind that colleges, even the Ivies, have to admit significantly more students than the number they have planned for their incoming freshman class size, because not every student who is admitted ends up attending. *But* the more students are admitted under early decision, the fewer need to be admitted during the regular cycle because the school already knows that 40 to 50 percent of the class is committed and coming. The school's selectivity index improves, as well as the yield index, which measures those students who have been accepted and choose to enroll. Early decision improves the yield index because the college is guaranteed that a certain number of students will attend.

➡ **Competing for applicants.** Colleges want to attract applicants, and a reputation for giving admissions preference to students in the ED pool may do just that. The Kennedy School study suggests that if a student knows that between two comparable schools, one institution is more lenient in its standards of admission with its ED pool of applicants than the other, he might opt for the one that gives preference to early decision applicants.

Is Early Decision Right for You?

So early decision is good for colleges, but is it good for you?

The decision to apply early decision to a college should not be made lightly. It's binding. If the school admits you, you agree to withdraw any other applications and enroll in that school the following September.

There are advantages and disadvantages to this admissions option. Consider them carefully before checking the box marked early decision on the application.

Advantages

☞ The rate of admission for early decision candidates at most colleges is higher than for the regular applicant pool. For example, Yale admitted 37 percent of its ED applicants and only 16 percent of the regular applicant pool. Most schools would argue that is because the ED pool has exceptionally large numbers of qualified students. The website of Muhlenberg College (Allentown, Pennsylvania) states: "Last year, we admitted 35 percent of our applicants overall, but 60 percent of the ED candidates. We are simply more willing to take a chance on the student who is more committed to Muhlenberg."

☞ You may improve your chances of admission. Students who are qualified but may not necessarily stand out in the regular pool may have an advantage when being considered in the ED pool. The Kennedy School study found that "the admissions effect of applying early is approximately equal to a 100 point increase in SAT score." This study analyzed five years' worth of admissions data at 14 select colleges and found that students were admitted to the colleges from the early decision applicant pool at a rate similar to students with SAT scores 100 points higher but who were in the regular decision pool. Skidmore College in Saratoga Springs, New York, makes it clear:

> A slightly higher percentage of the early decision pool is accepted compared with the regular decision pool due to the nature of the first-choice commitment involved in early decision. Also, an early decision candidate competes in a pool of several hundred applicants as opposed to several thousand for regular decision. As a selective college, Skidmore receives applications from more qualified students than can be accepted. A qualified candidate for admission does have a statistically better chance for admission through early decision, but that should not be what drives the decision to apply early.

Note: Skidmore admits that it likes the fact that the applicant has made Skidmore her first choice and rewards that with preferential treatment. It's not a guarantee of admission, but it does clearly help.

- Some schools will only give preference to children of alumni if the student applies early decision. If the student applies regular decision, he is given no special preference.

- If accepted, you are finished with the college admissions process by mid-December, relieving the stress of senior year.

Disadvantages

- You are locked in to a school early in your senior year, and some studies have indicated that your choices may change as you mature over the year. Harvard University admissions director Marilyn McGrath Lewis points out "We know from experience that there is a fair number of students who apply somewhere early and in the end want to go somewhere else. We think most people need the benefit of their senior year." You are locked into a school even if your choice of major has changed and the school doesn't offer it!

- Your financial aid package may be affected. This is an issue that schools are examining, but if you need to be able to compare aid packages, ED may not be right for you. See Chapter 9 for a more detailed discussion about financial aid.

- You may make a decision on your first choice college based on strategy, not preference. Some students sacrifice their dreams of attending a certain college because they think it's not worth the risk of "wasting" an early decision preference. Given that all competitive colleges admissions are iffy and without any guarantee of success, maximizing your chances—even if it means substituting a first-choice school for one you think is more likely to accept you—is a choice students must confront.

- "Senioritis" may strike early. If accepted early decision, some students "check out" of high school, paying little attention to classes and courses.

- If you are rejected in December, it hurts more than in April. Robert Sweeney, a guidance counselor at Mamaroneck High School, New York, points out that students who get a rejection or deferral from their early decision college have nothing to counterbalance the disappointment. There's no competing good news. In contrast, assuming students have chosen their college list well and included several safety schools, disappointing letters in April are offset by several letters of admission.

So Are You Ready?

It's easy to get sucked into the early decision game. And the stats seem to back up the premise that there is an advantage to applying to a school early decision. But don't forget that even those colleges that accept 50 percent of their class ED still accept the other 50 percent from the regular decision pool. If you are not ready to make the commitment, if you feel that you need to be able to compare financial aid packages, or if you have been deferred or rejected by your ED school, you will still get into college. It may not be the school to which you have applied early decision, but remember your original list of colleges. Although you may have preferred one place, any of them would be acceptable to you. And one of them will accept you.

Before you apply early decision, can you truthfully answer yes to the following?

- I *know* I will be happy to attend this college.
- This college has the characteristics I want and the majors that interest me.
- I've looked carefully at other schools, and this college is the place I most want to spend the next four years.

If the Answer Is Yes to Early Decision

An early decision application takes work.

1. You need to complete all the paperwork by November 1 (or 15)—a good six weeks before the more common January 1 deadline.
2. Ideally, you will have completed all your standardized testing the spring before, but should you need to take or retake any tests, you will have to rush your scores (for an additional fee) so they can be considered in time for the ED application pool.

3. As soon as possible, give your teachers and counselor the forms for their letters of recommendation as well as the date the paperwork is due. The same is true for any other people who are writing additional letters of reference for you.

4. *Important:* You must start to prepare the rest of your college applications. There is no guarantee of admission for anyone to any college. Should you be deferred or rejected, you will have less than a month to complete the rest of your college applications in order to meet a January 1 deadline. Check out the questions on the remaining applications and begin formulating answers to any essays you will need to write. While you may be able to adapt some of the written responses you used on your ED application, you will have to tailor some of your answers specifically to each college application. You don't want to have to all this work at a time when you are disappointed and possibly depressed that you didn't get accepted to your ED school. Remember that more applicants are deferred or rejected than accepted. Plan ahead—it's bad luck to be over-confident about an early decision offer of admission.

The Second Cycle of Early Decision

This is a relatively new phenomenon—but one that is becoming increasingly more popular among selective schools—that extends the early decision option. The deadline for the second cycle is usually in late December or mid-January, although some schools extend that into February. The point is to catch those students who either were unwilling to commit earlier to a single school, or more likely, were deferred or rejected from their first ED school. Skidmore College offers two early decision cycles. The first deadline is December 1, with an answer by January 1; the second deadline is January 15, with an answer by February 15.

Remember: You will have to complete the applications to your full list of colleges because their deadlines can't wait until you have heard from the second cycle of ED. But you can decide to mark one school as early decision (second cycle), and then if you are accepted, you will have to withdraw your other applications from consideration.

The second cycle of early decision is still just as binding as the first early decision cycle. It's a balancing act of getting the advantages of ED mentioned earlier versus taking your chances to see which schools admit you, giving you the chance to choose from a larger group in April.

What Are My Chances of Acceptance If I've Been Deferred in Early Decision?

It depends on the institution. Skidmore College says it helps if an applicant has made clear that Skidmore is number one on her college list: "If deferred, they [applicants] will have effectively communicated their first-choice interest to the Admissions Committee as they are reevaluated through the regular decision process."

At other schools it's no help and may be a hindrance. Essentially, some colleges reason they gave you their best look in the ED pool, and unless you've earned a Pulitzer Prize in the meantime (and even then!), you are unlikely to be admitted in the regular decision pool.

Even so, should you be deferred, send a strong letter to the director of admissions restating that the college is your first choice and that you still hope to attend. Make sure your first semester grades are dynamite and are sent to your file with a letter that emphasizes how well you are doing in challenging senior-year classes. Be sure to send information about any new honors you have received, too.

Ask your guidance counselor to call the institution to get a read on your chances of admission in the regular decision pool. He may not get a definitive answer, but any feedback would be helpful in planning what to do next. One student, a nationally ranked fencer, was deferred from one of the Ivy League colleges in the early decision cycle. His guidance counselor checked with the admissions office and was told that the student had almost been admitted and would be seriously considered in the regular decision pool. The admissions officer added that the fencing coach had included him among prospective recruits, and this would be important in the regular decision cycle. This information was enough to stay the course. Although he had considered applying in the second cycle of early decision at another college, the student decided to take his chances. He sent in seven other applications for consideration in the regular decision pool. In April, he was admitted to the Ivy school that had been a first choice for him, and, ironically, deferred from the college he had considered as a second cycle ED choice. A happy ending, but, of course, there was no guarantee. It definitely had been a gamble.

Dealing with Disappointment

Getting deferred or rejected during the early decision cycle can be especially disappointing because there is nothing to counterbalance it. It can be frustrating because it means that a lot of work on regular applications needs to be done in a short period of time.

One student recalls his own experience. He was one of four classmates who had applied to the same college early decision, but he was the only one who was deferred. "I was devastated when I got the thin envelope. I didn't want to go to school and face everybody, especially when I found out that the other three kids all got in. But then I heard that the valedictorian of our class had also been deferred from her early decision school. I thought she had a lock on acceptance—but that taught me that nobody does." While you will undoubtedly be upset if you are deferred or rejected, you will also find that you are in good company. There are undoubtedly other people in your high school who were also not accepted.

You will also have to face the frustration of seeing some students get in when you thought you were better qualified. The college guidance counselor at a private elite school laughed when asked if she had been surprised at any of the early decision results of her students and said, "Yes, one girl got in that I frankly didn't expect. But then I discovered that her father was close friends with the chairman of the college's board of trustees." That's not a lock on admissions (see the following "Legacies" section), but in this case, it probably made the difference.

Bottom line: There will be some students who are admitted and some who are rejected, and you won't be able to understand the reasoning behind the decisions. It's not always a fair process.

Legacies

Are you related to someone who graduated from a college you are interested in attending? If so, you're called a *legacy* and may qualify for some preferential treatment! You may not get as much preference as you would like or as much as some people think you will, but being a legacy does help when admissions officers review your file.

Rule #1 to remember: Being a legacy won't get you into the school if you are not qualified. Even if your parents have contributed enough money to the college that there are several huge buildings on the campus with your family name over the door, it won't overcome a poor academic record. One alumni director of a well-endowed college insisted that a million-dollar donation isn't a guarantee of admissions, and anything less than that is always appreciated but not enough to sway an admissions officer. Clemson University, South Carolina, warns, "While legacy is a factor in the admissions decision, it does not replace the importance of academic credentials." The alumni director of one of the Ivies told me that even the child of the chairman of the university's board of trustees was turned down for admission.

Basically it's up to each college to determine who they want to consider as a legacy application. For Columbia University, New York, you need to have a parent who graduated from the undergraduate college. For other institutions, like Clemson, "Questions about family members (father, mother, sister, brother, spouse) who have attended Clemson are included on the application for admission and are considered in the review of the application." For other institutions, like Cornell University, Ithaca, New York, a legacy is considered to be the child or grandchild of a graduate of the university's undergraduate *or* graduate schools. Some schools give some preference if a sibling of a current student applies. As one alumni director explains, "The assumption is that the siblings had similar academic preparation for college and that the younger one will be able to handle the challenges the university has to offer."

Bottom line: Ask admissions officers how their school defines legacy.

Your Parents' Role

Your parents don't have to be major financial contributors to their alma mater(s) for you to get extra attention from the admissions office. As one alumni director described it, "All applications are read by at least two admissions officers, but legacy applicants are read for a third time with that in mind." The process may differ from college to college, but the underlying premise is the same: a respect for the children of alumni. That said, however, Dean Stetson of the University of Pennsylvania points out that only about 40 percent of alumni children are admitted. Further, as noted, Penn only considers legacy for early decision applicants.

Another category of applicants also get special attention. These are the students who are on the list sent to the admissions office by the College's Office for Alumni Affairs. These are the offspring of active alumni volunteers. These individuals aren't just donors, but also volunteer their time for the college and serve on committees, fund-raising boards of the college, reunion committees, etc. They give of their time over a period of years. For example, one mother served as the chair of her class's twenty-fifth reunion. She worked effortlessly to solicit funds from her fellow graduates in honor of their reunion, and the class made a huge donation to the college. Two years later, this mom's son applied for admission. His standardized test scores were excellent, his extracurricular activities were strong, but his GPA was acceptable, not outstanding. Had he not had his mother's connection, he probably wouldn't have been admitted given his record. In fact, he was deferred when he applied for early decision but was then admitted in April. Most experts, looking just at his record, would have thought the student wouldn't have made the cut, but knowing his mother's active alumni role in the college, acknowledged that the admissions decision made more sense.

Bottom line: If your parents are actively involved in their alma mater(s), they should write a letter to the director of alumni affairs, noting that you have applied to the college. The letter should be a gentle reminder of your parents' active involvement, as well as your strong interest in the university.

If your family members are generous contributors to a school, *over a long period of time,* a note to the institution's director of development (fund-raising) is also appropriate. Multimillion-dollar donors to a college don't even have to be graduates of the institution to be included in the development office's list of applicants of special interest.

The applications from the offspring of large contributors to an institution often earn a second look, but money is no guarantee of admissions. For most families, their contributions, while appreciated, are not enough to merit preferential treatment by the university's office of development.

College Interviews

For some colleges, interviews are an important part of the admissions process. For example, Hamilton College, Clinton, New York, a small, liberal arts school, almost makes an interview a requirement: "Because the admission committee wants to know as much as possible about each applicant, **a personal interview is strongly recommended** [their emphasis]. Students who have not interviewed will be at a competitive disadvantage in the admission process." At Hamilton you can be interviewed on campus, or for those students who cannot visit the campus, you can arrange for an off-campus interview with an alumni representative. This type of interview would be *evaluative*—the school will use the interviewer's assessment of the candidate as part of the admissions process.

Other colleges see the interview as *informational.* The University of Pennsylvania limits on-campus interviews to applicants who are the children or grandchildren of alumni. It is basically a courtesy. Otherwise, all interviews are done off-campus by alumni. The interview is not required for admission and is intended to serve as "a valuable source for learning more about the University." Penn makes it clear to prospective students: "We encourage you to rely upon your application for admission as a forum for presenting the many unique aspects of your candidacy." The interview won't answer that purpose.

For others schools, the interview serves a combination of purposes. Hobart and William Smith College, Geneva, New York, another small liberal arts institution, views interviews as both "informative and evaluative. … Interviews are a great way for you to get to know Hobart and William Smith and for us to learn more about you. The interview, because it is personal, lets us assess whether or not you are a good match for us and lets you do the same."

And sometimes you have to read between the lines. Certainly, some schools try very hard to arrange for each applicant to be interviewed. At Macalester College in St. Paul, Minnesota, interviews are "strongly recommended, but not required." Not only can you be interviewed on campus, but during January the admissions staff visit major cities (Boston, Chicago, Washington, D.C., Denver, London, New York, Portland, San Francisco, Seattle, Stockholm, and Tokyo) and schedule interviews with applicants. If you don't live near one of the off-campus interview sites, you can meet with Macalester alumni closer to your home.

And other schools, like Emory University in Atlanta or Vanderbilt University in Nashville, Tennessee, don't interview at all.

Whether or not the college places a great deal of weight on the results of the interview, you want to make a good impression. Even for schools that place little importance on interviews, one representative pointed out, "I'm not sure how much a good interview helps, but I know that a bad one can affect an application."

Bottom line: Ask the admissions officer at each college, or check the institution's website, to determine the institution's policy regarding interviews. Even if the college doesn't require an interview, it's wise to ask for one. Just requesting an interview, whether on-campus or off-, gives the college a strong signal of your interest. That's valuable just by itself.

How to Ace an Interview

Like applying for a job, a college interview is your opportunity to impress the institution's representative with your talents and interest, so you need to prepare for each interview. Here's how:

1. **Call early for an appointment.** Some schools will schedule interviews for prospective students as early as February of your junior year. Remember that most schools get inundated with requests, especially over holiday weekends in the fall. Plan ahead.

2. **Conduct a practice interview.** Some high schools hold "mock" college interviews so students can become more comfortable with the process. If yours does not, ask a parent or a friend to rehearse with you. While you don't want to sound like you are reading from a script, you should practice your answers and questions (see the following "What Happens at the Interview?" section).

3. **Do your homework.** Read the college's website and check the catalog and other material sent to prospective students. Watch the school's video or take the online virtual tour if one is available. You don't want to ask obvious questions that can be easily answered from printed material.

4. **Impressions count.** Remember, this is just like an interview for an office job. Dress neatly and conservatively:

   ☞ *For men:* Dress pants and shirt, tie (optional), and blazer. Shave before the interview.

   ☞ *For girls:* Dress pants or skirt or dress (not too short or too bare).

   No T-shirts with "out there" messages. No tank tops or shorts. As one alum interviewer noted, "Lose the nose ring." Also, don't chew gum or play with the objects in the room.

5. **Arrive at least five minutes early.** The interviewer may have scheduled several appointments to meet prospective students. Arrive early so that she can keep to schedule, but if it's a private home, don't arrive too early to ensure privacy for other applicants.

6. **Watch your words.** Don't use slang or swear words. Be polite, even if you disagree with the interviewer. You are trying to impress the interviewer with your poise and demonstrate that you are articulate and thoughtful. Don't hesitate to express an opinion. You want to let the interviewer know that you are intelligent. On the other hand, don't deliberately try and provoke the interviewer just for the sake of argument.

7. **Make eye contact and offer a firm handshake.** Look the interviewer in the eye. That shows respect and a level of confidence. A firm handshake is also a sign of confidence—and you'll need it when you go on job interviews.

8. **Go alone.** If your parents are going to accompany you to the interview, have them wait for you in the car or nearby. This is a small sign to the interviewer that you are independent enough to handle college life.

9. **Say thank you.** Send a short thank you note after the interview. Tell the interviewer you appreciate the time he spent with you, that you learned a lot about XX college, and that you are very interested in enrolling in XX college.

What Happens at the Interview?

A college interview is a give-and-take session. *Plan ahead.* Walk into the interview ready to answer some questions. Take time to collect your thoughts before answering, and don't be afraid of a little silence. You want to say what you mean, not just what's on the tip of your tongue. There are no right or wrong answers to these typical interview questions:

- **Why do you want to attend this college?** Be specific. For example, mention classes or majors that interest you, the location if that is important to you, the size of the school, the diversity of the student body, the breadth of extracurricular activities, OR the strength of the sports program.

- **Do you have a major in mind?** Don't worry if you haven't selected a major yet. One admissions officer noted that the most popular major of incoming freshmen is "I don't know," followed closely by "I changed my mind." Be honest and say you haven't decided just yet, but then list some of your interests.

- **Do you know what you'd like to do when you finish college?** If you don't yet know your future career, that's okay. That's what going to college is supposed to help you decide. But you can talk in general about your interests.

- **What book really made an impression on you?** Talk about books that have intrigued you, challenged you, angered you, or really made you think. Don't try to second-guess what book will impress the interviewer. You'll speak more knowledgeably if you tell the truth about what you really liked. You can also add books that you read for fun—for example, if you like science fiction, tell the interviewer that as well. He may be sci-fi fan, too.

☞ **What interests you? What do you like to do in your free time?** Here's your opportunity to sell yourself and tell the school more about your nonacademic side. Convey your passion for theater, sports, art, music, politics, or whatever. Again, there is no right or wrong answer. Do make sure if you are talking about something you feel strongly about, that it is reflected on your application as well. It will not make sense if you claim something is very important to you and then fail to mention it on your application.

☞ **What courses are you taking in high school? What's your favorite?** You don't have to recite your high school transcript, but be sure to highlight any honors or AP classes. When you answer which class most interests you, also explain why. One student explained that one of her favorite classes wasn't because it was a subject she particularly enjoyed, but because the teacher made it interesting and challenging. That's okay, because colleges value good teaching and like the idea that a student would be willing to take a class simply to have a strong teacher.

☞ **What other colleges are you applying to?** This is a tough question to answer because you need to be honest that there are other schools on your list, and at the same time, make it clear that you are really interested in this particular college. Don't say this college is your first choice unless that is true. But do stress that you really hope to attend this institution and cite some of the reasons.

The interviewer will ask if you have any questions or concerns, so have some questions in mind to ask. You want to avoid asking questions that can be easily answered by reading the brochures and catalog, though. Here are some sample questions to ask:

☞ What was most meaningful to you about attending XX college? (This is a good question for alumni interviewers. It's an opportunity for them to tell you what they thought was special about their alma mater.)

☞ Are there many research opportunities for undergraduates?

☞ Are undergraduates generally able to get into their first-choice classes? How about for freshmen and sophomores?

- Are professors accessible?

- How close are town-gown relations? Do students become involved in local politics? Soup kitchens? Community affairs?

Common Application

You can make your life easy—or you can do it right.

The Common Application is a single form that is accepted by 227 institutions, including Harvard. Some schools accept the Common Application but then send the student a supplemental form requesting additional information or essays. But the concept is supposed to simplify your life. You need only complete this one application, photocopy it, send it and the appropriate application fee to as many colleges as you like, then sit back and wait for your answers.

The Common Application is available online at www.commonapp.org, or you can get a copy of the application from your high school guidance office. Colleges that agree to accept the application pledge to accept it "without prejudice." That is, schools are supposed to consider equally prospective students who use the institution's own applications and those who use the Common Application.

Specifically, the National Association for College Admission Counseling have passed a resolution that states ...

College and university members will not discriminate in the admission selection process against applicants based on the particular application form that an applicant uses, provided that the college or university has agreed explicitly, as in common application membership, or implicitly, as in online or other computer-based technology, to accept the particular version of the application.

From the NACAC Statement of Principles of Good Practice.

Having said all that, don't use the Common Application if you can help it. It's so easy now to use the institution's own application, which is almost always available online. In fact, some schools, like Hiram College in Hiram, Ohio, waive the application fee if you apply online. Using the school's own application says something important to the college. It says you took the time and effort to use their form or that you went to the website or wrote away for the application. It takes very little time, but using the school's application makes a strong statement about your commitment.

On the other hand, some schools use the Common Application instead of developing their own. Of course, under those circumstances, you'll use the Common Application.

Bottom line: Take the time to read the college's website or printed material. If they provide their own application form, use it.

Supplemental Materials

You may choose to enrich your application with portfolios or tapes. If you are going to do so, make sure your supplemental is of professional quality. For example, John Murray, AP art teacher at Mamaroneck High School in Mamaroneck, New York, helps his students prepare their portfolios by taking slides of their work throughout the fall of their senior year. That way they can include professional-level photographs of their artwork with their college applications. Murray encourages all his AP students—not just students applying to design school—to include an art portfolio with their application. It clearly indicates the breadth and depth of one of their passions.

Similarly, the head of the music department at a high school said she encourages seniors to include a tape of their voice or instrumental participation with their application.

But let's be realistic. College admissions officers read thousands of applications in a limited period of time. If you are going to submit additional material, make sure it is clear to the reader, from your application, what the material is and why it's important to understanding who you are.

One student had two inches left on his application after completing his essay. He'd already described his love of art and music in other parts of the application, so at the very bottom, he used the space to draw a cartoon of himself playing the drums. It made sense and left a good, strong impression on the reader!

Ethnic or Racial Preferences

College applications include questions about your racial, ethnic, religious, and national heritage. These questions are generally optional, so you can choose whether or not to answer them. The whole area of affirmative action and racial preferences is controversial and unsettled. There are currently lawsuits before several courts contesting whether or not race may be used as a factor in the admissions process.

Most colleges defend these questions by stressing that they are interested in having a diverse student body. As an African American or Latino applicant, your racial heritage may strengthen your application. Schools that do value race or ethnicity as factors in admissions argue that these are just some of the many factors they consider in applications. They argue that other schools might seek to expand the geographic diversity of their student body and give preference to applicants from underrepresented states. But remember that there are many other variables that will go into the equation, including your academic record, standardized test scores, essays, recommendations, and extracurricular activities.

For Asian Americans, there is another side to the issue. An article by Kenneth Lee in *The New Republic* charged that some Asian students believe that their applications to elite universities were judged by a harder standard than other students. They point, for example, to a study at the University of California, Berkeley, which revealed that "the average Asian freshman in 1994 had an average SAT score of 1293 and a 3.9 GPA, compared to 1256 and 3.86 for whites and 3.43 and 994 for blacks."

Bottom line: If you belong to a racial or ethnic minority, talk to your guidance counselor about which schools might give some preference to your application. But don't expect miracles. Despite the inflammatory hype some anti–affirmative action activists promote, being a minority won't get you into a school if you don't meet the academic minimums. And don't forget that those minimums change for lots of students. Legacy applicants and recruited athletes often don't have the same SATs or GPAs that other applicants do. Remember that college admissions are, by definition, based on arbitrary decisions.

The Online Explosion

Many schools now offer students the opportunity to apply in several different ways. There is still the old-fashioned method of requesting an application, completing it, and mailing it back. But more and more institutions are allowing applications to be downloaded and submitted online. From the school's website, you can download an application and type in the requested information; or you can complete the application online, print it out, and mail it in; or you can complete the application online and forward it to the school electronically. Remember: If you apply to a college online, be sure and print out a copy of your application for your files.

A few schools are also beginning to notify applicants via e-mail or a page on their website of their admissions status. The schools continue to send the big or thin envelopes through the postal service. But notification via e-mail has its own potential for disaster. Harvard University sent out e-mail messages to its fall 2001 early action applicants (confirming letters were also sent via the U.S. Post Office); however, because of a software glitch, applicants who had AOL e-mail addresses did not receive their notices. The system was updated and revised for the spring applications. Yale University established a website that its early decision applicants could access to find out their status (confirming letters were also sent via the postal service). At this time, e-mail or website notification is still used as an adjunct to the postal service system.

Application Do's and Don'ts

Before you send off your application, either online or through the postal service, make sure you check for the following:

- Did you read all the directions on the application and follow them as instructed?
- Did you sign the application and enclose the application fee (or if you are applying online, follow the procedures indicated for fee payment)?

- Did you proofread your application at least twice—and then have someone else proofread it, too?
- Have you given your teachers the recommendation forms, along with stamped, addressed envelopes? Similarly, have you given your guidance counselor his form along with the mid-year evaluation form?
- Have you sent all your standardized test results?
- Have you made photocopies of all applications?

Add to Your College Box

Some schools send out postcards when your application file is complete (with all necessary standardized test scores, recommendations, etc.). Keep any confirmation letters such as these as well as photocopies of all your college applications in your College Box.

What You Need to Know

- Early decision applications may be popular, but you need to make sure that you are ready to make the commitment required if you are accepted.
- Legacy and affirmative action may play a role in the admissions process, but both are factors that must be supported by other elements of the application.
- You need to prepare for a college interview, much as you prepare for a job interview.
- Proofread your applications several times, and have someone else review them as well. Then mail them off and relax! It's out of your hands now.

Chapter 9

Financial Aid 101

Coming Up in This Chapter

- Comparing financial aid packages to get the best offer
- Get the aid you need with work-study programs—without incurring additional debt
- Are early decision applications the best option for students who need financial aid?
- Merit-based scholarships: good for colleges wanting to attract strong students and good for students looking for a good education at a reduced cost

College costs big bucks. According to the College Board ...

- The average yearly cost of a four-year *public* college or university is $3,754.
- The average yearly cost of a four-year *private* college or university is $17,123.

And it's only going up. Currently, college costs have been increasing between 5 to 6 percent per year. If you need financial aid, you're in good company. At public colleges and universities, more than 60 percent of students receive financial aid; at private schools, that number soars to more than 75 percent.

This chapter can't begin to cover all the ins and outs of financial aid. Its purpose is to give you leads on some great resources that offer inside information on how to navigate the financial aid maze.

Financial Facts

The College Board reports that ...

- Only 6 percent of all students attend colleges that cost more than $24,000 per year.

- Public two-year colleges, where the average tuition is less than $2,000 per year, attract 45 percent of all students.

- The tuition bill for almost 70 percent of students attending four-year colleges is less than $8,000.

- There's more financial aid available than ever before: $74.4 billion.

Let's Define the Terms

Campus-based programs   These are U.S. Department of Education federal student aid programs, like the Federal Perkins Loan, Federal Supplemental Educational Opportunity Grant (FSEOG), and Federal Work-Study, which are administered by colleges.

College Scholarship Service/Financial Aid PROFILE   This is the financial aid application service of the College Board. It supplements the FAFSA (Free Application for Federal Student Aid) and is used by 450 colleges and universities, as well as 350 scholarship programs. While you can receive state and federal aid just by completing the FAFSA, some colleges require the CSS/PROFILE in order to receive institutional money. You can apply online at www.collegeboard.com or through a form requested from the College Board.

Consolidation loan   This aid combines one or more of your federal loans (Stafford, PLUS, SLS, FISL, Perkins, Health Professional Student Loans, NSL, HEAL, Guaranteed Student Loans) into one new direct loan from a single lender. How does this help? It reduces the amount of your monthly payment by extending the term of your loan beyond the 10-year repayment plan. Some loans can be extended up to 30 years, but this means that the amount of interest you will eventually pay is increased.

Direct loan   A federal program that permits schools to act as the lending agency and manage the loan funds directly. Monies are from the federal government, but not all schools participate.

Expected Family Contribution (EFC)   This is how much you and your parents are expected to pay toward your education. The amount depends on family earnings, assets, how many students in college, and family size, and doesn't necessarily correlate with the reality of how much your family can actually afford to contribute. In order to get an EFC, you must file a FAFSA.

FAFSA (Free Application for Federal Student Aid)   This is the application that students and parents must complete for almost all forms of student aid. It's available at high schools and colleges, online at www.fafsa.cd.gov, or by calling 1-800-4-FEDAID (1-800-433-3243).

Federal Direct Student Loan Program (FDSLP)   These federal loans are provided to you and your parents through your college.

Federal Family Education Loan Program (FFEL)   These federal loans are provided to students through private lenders such as banks, credit unions, and savings and loans.

Federal Stafford Loan   Federally guaranteed loan with low interest. There are two kinds of Stafford Loans: subsidized, which are awarded on a need basis, and unsubsidized, which are nonneed-based. For both types, you can defer payment until you are out of school, but for unsubsidized loans, interest accrues while you are still in school. However, you can defer paying the interest until you graduate. All students are eligible for an *unsubsidized* Stafford Loan, regardless of income; however, you must first file a FAFSA.

Federal Work-Study   Federally sponsored program that pays some of the student's salary for part-time school-year employment in school departments or businesses. Eligibility is need-based.

Grant   Aid that does not have to be paid back.

Merit-based aid   Nonneed-based aid given on the basis of artistic, academic, athletic, or other criteria. This aid normally does not have to be paid back, but it may have certain restrictions or requirements (such as maintaining a certain GPA) in order to continue.

Pell Grant   Federal grant program. Aid that does not have to be paid back.

Perkins Loan   Need-based federal loan program with low interest rates.

PLUS (Parent Loans for Undergraduate Students) Loan   Federal loan that permits parents to borrow up to the difference between what the education costs and what the financial aid package covers. Parents must begin repayment of loans within 60 days after disbursement. The life of the loan can be spread out over many years in order to reduce the monthly payments, but this increases the total amount repaid because of the accrual of interest.

Scholarship   Financial aid that does not have to be repaid.

Subsidized loan   Aid on which students do not have to pay interest on until the grace period expires.

Title IV Programs   This is a group of federal student aid programs that includes Pell Grants, Federal Supplemental Educational Opportunity Grants, Federal Work-Study, Federal Perkins Loans, Federal Stafford Loans, Federal PLUS Loans, Direct Loan, Direct PLUS Loan, and SSIG.

Unsubsidized loan   A loan on which interest accrues while the student is still in school.

Let's Get Started: Organization Is the Key

The Internet has changed the financial aid search. Online databases allow you to surf your way to aid money. But don't let the technology fool you—it still takes time, effort, and creativity to find the dollars you need to reduce your college financial load. Whether you are searching for financial aid based on demonstrated need or a merit scholarship to help defray the costs, organization is the key.

Get a separate box to keep all your financial aid forms and information together. And you can't just toss all the paperwork into the box. You need to make separate file folders for each scholarship program to which you apply. Each one has a separate timetable that must be carefully met.

To help stay on top of all your financial aid paperwork ...

- Mark on the front of each scholarship folder the due date, contact person, and a checklist of items needed to complete the form, which you can check off as you complete them. Keep a photocopy of the completed application in the folder.

- Set up a calendar and mark due dates for each application.

- Arrange for necessary recommendations early in the process. Provide your references with the necessary forms and stamped envelopes. Later, write a thank you note to each person who wrote recommendations for you.

- Write, proof, *and proof again* all information—especially essay and contest entries.

What Kind of Aid Are You Looking For?

There are two kinds of financial aid: merit-based and need-based.

Merit-based aid is in the form of scholarships and does not require you to pay it back, but you may be expected to maintain a certain grade point average. For merit-based aid, no financial disclosures are necessary.

You may want to try to get some merit scholarship money because ...

- You've been told that you don't qualify for need-based aid.

- You've received some need-based aid but it's not enough.

- Like most people, you want to reduce the exorbitant cost of higher education!

Need-based aid can come in the form of scholarships and loans. For this type of aid, your parents will have to complete a variety of forms that detail your family's financial situation, and include their most recent tax information.

Demonstrating Need

Seven out of ten full-time students receive some form of aid. Two thirds of the grants and loans distributed each year are based on need. Most families can prove some need—at least for low-interest loans—and 60 percent of aid is in the form of these types of loans.

Merit-Based Scholarships

Here's a great deal! Merit-based scholarships don't have to be paid back and are not calculated based on financial need. Schools use these scholarships to attract students who might otherwise choose another institution. The amount of merit scholarships distributed increased 97 percent between 1989 and 1995. (Need-based scholarships increased 114 percent.) To qualify, you have to have something schools want, for example, you improve their student profile because your GPA or standardized test scores are higher than the average of the institution's incoming freshmen, or you have an outstanding musical talent and will enrich the college's band or orchestra.

Scholarships can range from an honorarium of a few hundred dollars to a completely free ride. At Washington University in St. Louis, Missouri, about 10 percent of the freshman class received merit scholarships. These scholarships range from half of the tuition costs to full tuition plus a stipend toward room and board.

Franklin and Marshall College in Lancaster, Pennsylvania, offers several merit scholarships. The Rouse Scholarship, awarded to no more than two incoming F&M students in each class, covers all academic costs, including full tuition, books, and lab fees. Rouse Scholars also receive Macintosh computers and are eligible to apply for a $3,000 research/travel grant. This scholarship can be renewed for three years, assuming the recipient meets certain academic requirements and demonstrates leadership at the college. The John Marshall Scholarship, awarded to select freshmen applicants, is a $12,500 merit-based scholarship renewable for all four years at the college (subject to the student maintaining a specified

GPA and making regular progress toward graduation), a computer, and the opportunity to apply for a maximum of $3,000 to cover expenses related to research, creative arts, or community and public service during their college career. Presidential Scholarships, also merit-based, grant recipients $7,500 per year, renewable for all four years of college.

Schools have the option of combining merit-based scholarships with need-based aid packages. For example, if an incoming student has a demonstrated need of $12,000 but is also eligible, based on her academic record, for merit scholarship of $5,000, the award may be limited to a total of just $12,000. The merit scholarship money is used to reduce the loan expectations of a typical aid package and student employment requirements.

Merit scholarships are subjective. Each school decides how much they want to offer. You may be worth more to one school than to another. Frankly, it comes down to how well you stack up against the competition for that spot at the school. You may be worth full tuition to one college and worth only half tuition to another.

Bottom line: If you are applying for need-based aid, ask the financial aid office if you are also eligible for merit scholarships and whether you need to submit separate applications for them.

Need-Based Aid Isn't Necessarily Free

If you are awarded financial aid based on need, the money will probably be primarily in the form of low-cost loans. You may receive some straight scholarship funds, but most aid packages have a big loan component. Although that means that you will have to repay these loans, the interest rate is comparatively low. If you receive federal *subsidized* loans, the interest doesn't start accruing until you're out of school. If you receive *unsubsidized* loans, the interest begins while you are still in school. *For both kinds of loans, you don't have to start paying them back until you're out of school.*

Your parents may borrow some of the funds through the Federal PLUS program. These loans are in your parents' name, and they are responsible for repayment. One advantage of PLUS Loans is that you can extend the payments for 10 years or longer. Of course, the longer you extend the life of a loan, the greater the amount of interest you will pay.

Work-Study Appeal

Some of your aid package may be in the form of Work-Study. The Federal Work-Study Program provides jobs for students with financial need. Some Work-Study jobs are on campus in college departments or offices. Off-campus Work-Study jobs are usually for a private nonprofit organization or a public agency, and the work performed must be in the public interest. Some colleges have agreements with private for-profit employers, but the job must be judged to be relevant to your course of study. Working off-campus may require travel, so you'll need to know how you will get to the job site. Do you have a car? If not, is there public transportation available? You'll also need to factor travel time into your schedule.

At the very least, you will be paid the current federal minimum wage, but it may be higher, depending on the type of work you do and the skills required. Your total Work-Study award depends on when you apply (because there are limited funds), your level of need, and the funding level of the college. As an undergraduate, you'll be paid by the hour; graduate students are sometimes paid a salary. Under Federal Work-Study, you can't be paid by commission or fee. The college has to pay you at least once a month, but depending on their accounting practices, it can be weekly or bi-weekly. You will be paid directly, unless you request that the college direct deposit your payments into your bank account or use the money to pay for tuition, fees, or room and board.

You can only work a limited number of hours, because you can't earn more than your total Federal Work-Study award. When assigning work hours, your employer or financial aid administrator will consider your class schedule and your academic progress.

The advantage to Work-Study funds is they do not have to be repaid. However, the problem with Work-Study funds is that you are paid for work that you have completed. It's a job, and you are paid on a weekly (or bi-weekly) basis throughout the school year. You may find yourself in a cash crunch until you get your first check.

Bargains on Loan Forgiveness

You can also reduce your amount of education debt by working in certain fields or joining certain service programs, for example ...

AmeriCorps and Volunteers in Service to America (VISTA)
1-800-942-2677

www.americorps.org

This is a national volunteer service agency. In exchange for 12 months of service, you will receive up to $4,725 toward loan repayment. In addition, if you are eligible, AmeriCorps will pay the interest that accrues during your service. Check with your lender.

Peace Corps
1-800-424-8580

www.peacecorps.org

With your lender's approval, your student loans (Stafford Loans, Perkins Loans, Federal Consolidation Loans, and Direct Loans) will be deferred during your two years of Peace Corps service. Students with Perkins Loans can receive a 15 percent cancellation of their loan for each year of service up to two years for a total of no more than 30 percent.

Teachers
Department of Education

www.ed.gov/offices/OSFAP/Students/repayment/teachers/perkins.html

You may be eligible for cancellation of up to 100 percent of your student loans if you teach ...

- In an elementary school or secondary school that serves low-income students.

- In a school system that has a shortage of teachers in a designated subject.

- In an elementary or secondary school operated by the Bureau of Indian Affairs (BIA) or operated on Indian reservations by Indian Tribal groups under contract with BIA to qualify as schools serving low-income students.

For the first two years, your loan cancellation rate is 15 percent per year. For the third and fourth years of service, the rate goes to 20 percent per year, and the remaining 30 percent balance is canceled at the end of the fifth year.

Stafford Loans up to $5,000 are also now eligible for loan cancellation in exchange for teaching five consecutive, complete school years in low-income schools.

There are other Perkins/NDSL cancellation provisions for Head Start, nurses or medical technicians, military personnel serving in areas of imminent danger, or certain types of law enforcement, family service, or early intervention work.

Loan forgiveness is also sometimes used as a recruitment tool in private industry, especially in professions or organizations that are short-staffed.

The Problem with Financial Aid and Early Decision Applications

If you need financial aid to help pay for college, an early decision application may not be your best course of action. Here's why: Each institution puts together its own aid package. So if you apply regular decision to three colleges, you may get three different aid packages.

For example, based on FAFSA, it's determined that you need at least $12,000 in financial aid. With your regular decision applications to three colleges, you get three aid packages:

- ✏ College A offers you the $12,000 as 60 percent loans, 20 percent Work-Study, and 20 percent scholarship.
- ✏ College B's package is 60 percent scholarship dollars (which do not have to be paid back), 20 percent loans, and 20 percent Work-Study.
- ✏ College C offers 80 percent as scholarships, 10 percent as loans, and 10 percent as Work-Study.

If you feel equally about all three colleges, you may decide that College C is the best choice for you because you will emerge after four years with the least amount of debt (assuming the aid package continues).

College Debt Timeline

Forty-five percent of college students have student loans averaging $18,363. It takes about seven years to pay off college loans.

But let's assume that you really like College A the best but are troubled by the amount of loans you will have to repay when you graduate. You could approach the financial aid office of College A with your competing offers and ask if they can improve their package. It's a little like shopping for a new car and comparing prices between competing dealerships. While the college may be unwilling or unable to change its financial aid offer, many schools do improve their packages after looking at what else the student is being offered by the competition.

Most colleges have an appeals process. Most schools will deny that they are willing to compete against other offers; however, that's exactly what often happens for incoming freshmen. In fact, Carnegie Mellon University in Pittsburgh, Pennsylvania, invites admitted students to fax in their other offers. Half of those students who responded had the amount of their aid increased an average of $3,000.

But with early decision, you don't have any competing offers. You only apply to one school and have to accept the financial aid offered, although you can appeal and ask for a review of the package. Should you decide to apply early decision and you know you will need financial aid, talk to the admissions office about the issue.

Here are some examples of the different ways colleges approach early decision and financial aid:

- At Carleton College in Northfield, Minnesota, "For those students who apply early decision, a tentative award will be included with the offer of admission. This award is based on estimated figures from the previous year, and may or may not change when actual figures are used."
- At Bates College in Lewiston, Maine, early decision candidates must submit a CSS/PROFILE at the time of application. This gives the college the information it needs to make an estimated award until a final decision can be made based on the FAFSA (which is due after January 1).

211

- Lafayette College in Easton, Pennsylvania, says, "Lafayette **guarantees** [their emphasis] to meet the demonstrated financial need of students admitted under the Early Decision Plan. ED applicants may submit the CSS/PROFILE as early as October using estimated information, **but no later than two weeks after the application for admission or Early Decision agreement has been received by the College** [their emphasis]. ED applicants must also file the FAFSA by February 1."

- Franklin and Marshall College offers ED candidates "an 'early read' of their financial aid application. Students are informed of a range of need-based financial aid prior to committing to F&M through an ED application."

- Johns Hopkins University, Baltimore, Maryland, makes a strong case for ED applicants: "As an Early Decision candidate, you are at an advantage for financial aid because you are the first to be considered for assistance. If you are accepted early decision to Hopkins and qualify for aid, you will receive a tentative aid offer based on past financial statements and current estimates. A firm aid offer will follow in the spring, pending receipt of your Free Application for Federal Student Aid (FAFSA) and the most current federal income tax returns. Unless the information provided on your FAFSA and tax returns varies significantly from original estimates, your financial aid package will remain unchanged."

  Hopkins then advises: "If we are unable to offer you adequate need-based financial aid, you may be released from the early decision contract. Because no additional need-based aid would be available to you as a regular decision candidate, your application will also be removed from consideration altogether."

Bottom line: Early decision may not be the best option if you need financial aid for college. But should you opt to become an ED applicant, check with the college's financial aid office for clear advice on your aid package.

Public vs. Private Colleges

If you need financial aid, don't assume that your only college option is a public institution. Although tuition and room and board are less expensive at public schools, private colleges are often better endowed and can offer more financial aid. You may find that when you compare aid packages, you are able to afford a private college.

Remember: Expected Family Contribution (EFC) remains the same whether you apply to a public or private institution. For families whose EFC is around $12,000, a private college may cost them the same as a public one. Here's how: With an EFC of $12,000, the family is unlikely to get any financial aid for a public institution because their contribution would cover tuition and other expenses. However, at a well-endowed private college, where tuition and room and board are calculated to be $21,000, while the EFC remains the same, the family can expect to get a financial aid package of $9,000 to make up the difference.

Bottom line: Choose the schools that interest you, whether public or private, and then compare the aid packages offered.

How Much Is a College Education Worth?

Even if you come out of college thousands of dollars in debt, it's worth it. According to the College Board, "people with a college degree earn 81 percent more on average than those with only a high school diploma." Over a lifetime, the gap in earnings potential between a high school diploma and a BA is more than $1,000,000.

Surfing the Web for Scholarship Money

Many websites offer you information on financial aid. Some have "calculators" to help you determine how much money you will need, and all have links to other resources on the web.

Check out the following websites when searching for scholarship money:

College Board
www.collegeboard.com

The financial aid section is just part of an extensive website devoted to college planning—and of course, standardized testing. The section on paying for college includes an overview of what you need to know about financial aid, specifics on forms that need to be completed for need-based aid, information on your financing options, help in comparing aid awards, data on loans, a scholarship search engine, and more.

Department of Education

www.ed.gov/prog_info/SFA/AstudentGuide
Federal Student Aid Information Center: 1-800-4-FED-AID (1-800-433-3243)

This is the federal government's website, which includes general information on financial aid as well as an online FAFSA. Be sure and read the "Bargains on Loan Forgiveness" section earlier in this chapter. Working in certain professions can significantly reduce your loan indebtness.

Educational Testing Service

www.ets.org

Basic information on financial aid offered here is part of a larger website from the premier testing organization and is linked with the College Board financial aid data. The ETS website offers information on financing a college education, application tips, borrowing for college, and hints for cutting college costs.

FinAid

www.finaid.org

This is a free, comprehensive, independent, and objective guide to student financial aid. It's a particularly strong site because it has a clear explanation of financial aid terms and a calculator program to help you figure out your needs. It also offers good links to a wide variety of websites that offer scholarships and loans. The extensive bibliography is especially good because not only does it list general financial aid books (of which there are dozens), but it also breaks down the books by subject so you can find information on scholarships available for specific disciplines, books on competitions and contests, books about writing, books for special populations such as disabled students and distance learners, books for studying abroad, and more.

Mapping Your Future

www.mapping-your-future.com

This site is sponsored by a group of agencies that participate in an important student loan program, Federal Family Education Loan Program (FFELP). You'll find especially helpful the explanation of student loans available.

U.S. News & World Report

www.usnews.com

The magazine website is extensive and helpful throughout the college selection process. The financial aid section includes information on using price as a factor in choosing a college; working as a student for money, skills, and fun; loan do's and don'ts; alternatives for when you are short on college funds; a scholarship search engine; tips on comparing aid packages; and more.

Wired Scholar

www.wiredscholar.com

Sponsored by Sallie Mae, the nation's leader in higher education finance, this is a comprehensive site that includes a schools search as well as a full discussion of the financial aid process from start to finish. You will find the various tools helpful for calculating long-term planning, college costs, future savings, monthly savings, monthly budget, repayments, and accrued interest. There is also a tool to estimate expected family contribution, which will help your parents estimate their potential financial responsibility before completing the FAFSA.

Register for The Wired Scholar monthly sweepstakes, a $1,000 scholarship awarded every month. One winner is selected from a pool of registered users. You can complete the registration form online or enter by mail: On a 4×6-inch card, type or legibly hand print the words "Wiredscholar Sweepstakes" along with your name, address, e-mail address (if you do not have an e-mail address, print "No e-mail address"), grade level, and telephone number, and mail to: Wiredscholar Sweepstakes Registration, 11600 Salliemae Drive MTC 2400, Reston, VA 20193.

The website also offers all the information in Spanish.

The following scholarship search engines are *free* to use. You enter your profile, and they match you to available scholarship opportunities.

FastWeb

www.fastweb.com

This the largest scholarship search engine on the Internet. You can explore more than 600,000 scholarships worth more than $1 billion. FastWeb has a reputation for being accurate and the most frequently updated of the Internet databases. You enter personal information, and it finds awards that fit your profile. Give FastWeb your e-mail address and it will notify you when new awards that match your profile are added to the database. This site also allows you to apply online for some awards. Plus there is a college search engine, and you can download applications for more than 700 colleges.

College Board

www.collegeboard.com

This is part of the comprehensive college site. In addition to the free search for scholarships, you'll also find information on loans, internships, and other financial aid programs from noncollege sources. College Board also offers suggestions on how to apply for a scholarship.

Scholarship Resource Network Express

www.srnexpress.com

This website offers a free search engine and a database of more than 8,000 programs with a distribution level of more than 150,000 awards worth more than $35 million. There are scholarships for everything from undergraduate education through postgraduate study.

Let the Army, Navy, or Air Force Foot the Bill

Why not let the U.S. government pay your way through college? Consider joining the Reserve Officers Training Corps (ROTC) program of one of the military services. ROTC programs are available at more than 1,000 colleges and universities. How much of a scholarship, how long you can keep it, what the requirements are to join and remain a member of ROTC, vary by the service.

All services offer some four-year scholarships that include full tuition, books, fees, and a monthly *tax-free* stipend. Some services offer health-related or Nurse ROTC scholarships. If your school doesn't have a ROTC program, you may be able to enlist at a nearby school through a cross-enrollment program. Schools like Tulane University in New Orleans, Louisiana, and Old Dominion University in Norfolk, Virginia, give free room and board to ROTC scholarship holders.

You don't have to pay back ROTC scholarships, but you will have to serve in the military for a few years in return. And your course load in college is heavier because in addition to your regular classes, you have to attend military science courses and participate in military labs, drills, and other practical training activities. Every summer, you will have to enter military service for a certain number of weeks.

For more information, contact the following:

Army ROTC
www.armyrotc.com
1-800-USA-ROTC (1-800-872-7682)

Navy ROTC
www.cnet.navy.mil/nrotc/nrotc.htm
1-800-USA-NAVY (1-800-872-6289)

Air Force ROTC
www.afoats.af.mil
1-800-522-0033, extension 2091

Financial Aid Myths

Have you heard the one about a scholarship just for left-handed students? Well, yes, there is one, but just one. You have to go to Juniata College in Huntington, Pennsylvania, to be eligible.

But more troubling is the myth that there are millions of scholarship dollars that go unclaimed each year. This legend is usually promoted by scholarship services that promise to get you on the inside track for these unclaimed aid dollars. The hitch is that you pay the service big bucks for work you can do yourself. And there is no way any of these services can guarantee you will get a scholarship. Save your money for college. Use the websites listed earlier in the chapter to start your own search. Talk to your guidance counselor for more information on local, state, and federal scholarships and loans available.

Specialized Scholarships

Although there is only one scholarship for being left-handed, thousands of dollars are distributed based on other specific qualifications. There are countless scholarships that are awarded just because you meet one of the following criteria:

- You are a member of a certain ethnic or religious group.
- You are a certain race or nationality.
- You are a man or a woman.
- You are majoring in a specific field.
- You or a family member belong to a service organization—or don't. For example, to be eligible for an Ambassadorial Scholarship from the Rotary Club, you cannot be a member of the organization.
- You are a member of Greek fraternity or sorority.
- You have a parent who is affiliated with a union or fraternal order.
- Your parent works for a company that provides scholarships to its employees.
- You are disabled.
- You are gay.

But like so much else about the financial aid process, it's up to you to find out what is available. There are books on scholarships (see Appendix A). Check the bulletin boards in your guidance counselor's office for local scholarship programs and contests you can enter, and stop by the financial aid office of the colleges you visit as well. There's also plenty of scholarship information available on the web, as mentioned in the earlier "Surfing the Web for Scholarship Money" section.

Be Alert for Scholarship Scams

The Federal Trade Commission cautions students to look and listen for these telltale lines used in scholarship frauds:

- **"The scholarship is guaranteed or your money back."** No one can guarantee that they'll get you a grant or scholarship. Look at the fine print. These refund guarantees have so many conditions or strings attached that it's almost impossible to get a refund. If you do sign up with one of these services, get refund policies in writing—before you pay.

- **"You can't get this information anywhere else."** That's simply wrong … and a tip-off about the likely quality and honesty of the service. There are lots of books to consult (see Appendix A) and free scholarship search engines on the Internet. Check out the public library and the financial aid office for more information on scholarships and grants, and ask your guidance counselor for help.

- **"I just need your credit card or bank account number to hold this scholarship."** This phrase signals real trouble. No organization that grants financial aid needs a credit card or bank account number to give you a scholarship or loan. And certainly, no one needs that information given to them over the telephone. The scam, sometimes, is that a shady company will ask for a checking account number to "confirm eligibility" and then debit the account without consent. Another scheme is for a company to quote a relatively small "monthly" or "weekly" fee and then ask for authorization to debit your checking account or credit card for an unlimited time period. With these types of companies, the only ones getting rich are the criminals.

- **"We'll do all the work."** If you need financial aid, there's no way around doing some work. You must apply for grants and scholarships yourself. Ask for help from reputable sources like your guidance counselor or from the financial aid offices of the colleges you're interested in attending.

- **"The scholarship will cost you some money."** By definition, a scholarship is free money to the recipient and doesn't cost anything.

- **"You've been selected" by a "national foundation" to receive a scholarship or "You're a finalist" in a contest you never entered.**

This is an instant red alert. Legitimate scholarship funds are never distributed this way. You can get the financial aid you need, but you must apply for the awards.

From the Federal Trade Commission:

If you attend a seminar on financial aid or scholarships, follow these steps:

- **Take your time.** Don't be rushed into paying for any services at the seminar. Avoid high-pressure sales pitches that require you to buy now or risk losing out on the opportunity. Solid opportunities are not sold through nerve-wracking tactics.

- **Investigate the organization you are considering paying for help.** Talk to a guidance counselor or financial aid advisor before spending your money. You may be able to get the same help for free.

- **Be wary of "success stories" or testimonials about extraordinary success.** The seminar operation may have paid "shills" to give glowing stories. Instead, ask for a list of at least three local families who've used the services in the last year. Ask each if they're satisfied with the products and services received.

- **Be cautious about purchasing from seminar representatives who are reluctant to answer questions or who give evasive answers to your questions.** Legitimate business people are more than willing to give you information about their service.

- **Ask how much money is charged for the service, what services will be performed, and what the company's refund policy is.** Get this information in writing. Keep in mind that you may never recoup the money you give to an unscrupulous operator, despite stated refund policies.

The FTC says many legitimate companies advertise that they can get students access to lists of scholarships in exchange for an advance fee. Other legitimate services charge an advance fee to compare a student's profile with a database of scholarship opportunities and provide a list of awards for which a student may qualify. **But you can enter your own profile into scholarship search engines and get the same information for free.**

If you've been ripped off by a shady "scholarship" program, you can file a complaint with the FTC by contacting the Consumer Response Center:

Consumer Response Center
Federal Trade Commission
600 Pennsylvania Avenue
Washington, DC 20580
1-877-FTC-HELP (1-877-382-4357)
www.ftc.gov (the online complaint form at the FTC website)

Although the FTC doesn't resolve individual problems for consumers, it can act against a company if it sees a pattern of possible law violations.

Bottom line: Legitimate companies never guarantee or promise scholarships or grants.

Things Sometimes Change

After you've applied for financial aid, stuff sometimes happens, such as a parent loses a job or a family member becomes ill. Although financial aid is granted on the basis of the previous year's income (as verified by income tax returns), in these circumstances, projections of family income can be changed and perhaps lead to an increase in financial aid. If something has changed your family's financial situation dramatically, contact the college's financial aid department directly. Be prepared to show appropriate documentation.

After You Get Your Award Letter

To compare financial aid offers, keep in mind that it's more than numbers. The dollar amounts may be the same, but how they are awarded may make a significant difference.

Ask yourself the following questions when comparing financial aid information:

- How much of the aid is in the form of loans? Scholarships? Work-Study?

- How will you meet the other expenses (such as books, room and board, and personal needs) of attending college?

- What are the terms of the aid package? Do you need to maintain a certain GPA? Are there other conditions to the aid?

- Will your transportation costs be higher if you attend a particular school?

- Does one package offer incentives such as a computer or special honors classes or seminars?

- How is the financial aid applied to college bills? Is it automatically deducted? If part of the aid is Work-Study, how much money will you need to pay the tuition bills that arrive before you begin working?

Bottom line: Ask your guidance counselor or the financial aid office of the colleges you are considering to help you compare aid packages.

Add to Your College Box

Get a new, separate box to keep all your financial aid forms and information together. Keep it with your College Box so you have all your college and financial aid papers close together.

What You Need to Know

- An early decision application may not be in your best interest if you need financial aid, because you won't be able to compare aid packages.

- Don't hesitate to appeal an aid package, especially if you can show a better offer from a competing school.

- Merit-based scholarship are available to students who can't demonstrate financial need.

- Be wary of scholarship search companies. They can't promise or guarantee funds, no matter what they say.

Chapter 10

Congratulations! You're In!

Coming Up in This Chapter

- ☞ Colleges will be checking your mid-year grades: how to avoid "senioritis"
- ☞ The acceptance letters have arrived!: how to make a final decision
- ☞ What you need to know to get out of wait-list limbo
- ☞ The paperwork has just begun: the forms that follow the acceptance letters

The applications are all in the mail. Now what? Is there anything else you can or should be doing? And once you get responses from the colleges you applied to, how do you choose among the ones that have accepted you? Then what?

In this chapter, I'll take you through the last stages of the college admissions process. When you get to the end, you can buy yourself a college T-shirt. You're almost there—you're in the home stretch.

Senioritis

Once college applications are in, it's tempting to slack off in school. A lot of kids do it. But don't. Your mid-year grades will definitely count when college admissions officers are reviewing your application. If you are taking AP and honor classes your junior and senior years, colleges will be able to judge how well you can handle the demands of college-level material. Your guidance counselor will send in those grades, and it will be your final opportunity to tell the admissions staff that you can handle the challenges ahead.

Bottom line: Make your senior year grades count. Work hard and give your counselor something to talk about.

There's no point in saying don't worry—because of course you're nervous about whether or not you will be admitted to your first-choice college. But keep in mind that you have put together a well-thought-out list of schools. You have included among your choices several safety schools so that—worse-case scenario—you will be accepted at one of the colleges you liked. Although you may prefer some colleges to others, each school in your group offers you the courses and campus culture that you want.

The (Thick) Envelope, Please!

It may be that all the schools you have applied to will report on the same day—but that is unlikely. Sometime in early March you'll begin to get your letters, hopefully of acceptance, but possibly of rejection or wait-listing.

But don't sit by your mailbox and wait. You may not get word via the U.S. Postal Service—or at least not at first. Schools are now beginning to use the Internet to advise students of their admissions decisions. Although you will get a follow-up letter (and materials), you may initially learn the decision either by accessing a website or via an e-mail message from the admissions office.

But in any case, the majority of colleges still respond with either the traditional thick or thin envelopes. And no college spends $2 or more on postage and supplies to tell you no, you didn't get in. So if you see a big envelope, congratulations! You're in!

If the letter is one of acceptance, the envelope will include other information you need to keep. It's time for another box! You absolutely must keep all the paperwork you will be receiving in the next few months. If you thought the application process was paper-intensive, wait until you see the acceptance process. You can toss any rejection letters into your original application box (or pitch them into the waste can), but keep the acceptance letters separate and accessible.

Pre-Frosh Days

Many colleges set aside a few days in April for prospective students to visit. These days are sometimes called Pre-Frosh Days. It's a chance to look the school over; meet other prospective students; check out the dorms, facilities, programs, and activities; and meet with faculty. There may be separate programs for parents on these days. This is the college's time to try and recruit you to enroll. If you can, take advantage of this opportunity, but keep it in perspective as well.

One student, torn between two schools, visited both during each college's Pre-Frosh Days. He stayed overnight in the dorms with other prospective students. His decision to choose one institution was solidified by the visit. As he explained, "I just felt more comfortable with the students I met at one college. I also was really impressed because [movie director] Oliver Stone was a guest speaker the night I was visiting." Some of this student's decision was based on gut instinct. Assuming you've done your homework when selecting schools and determined that the institutions offer the programs and majors you want, as well as the clubs and other activities you need, relying on your gut makes sense. You do want to be comfortable at the school where you're most likely to spend the next four (or more) years. But keep in mind that most schools will likely bring impressive guest speakers to campus during Pre-Frosh Days, so don't get too dazzled by the big-name stars. (That's what they want you to do.)

When on campus, talk most to students who currently attend the college, not the kids who, like you, are there as guests. You want to listen to currently enrolled students' feelings about the school—what they like and don't like. And although the admissions office will assign you to students who obviously like the college, take the time to seek out others in the student center, in the library, or on the quad who can give you a broad overview of the school. You want to know how upperclassmen—students who have been on campus for several years—feel about the college. For a small school, you want to be sure that the environment isn't too limiting. For a bigger school, you want to be sure that you won't feel lost or overlooked.

Bottom line: You've done your homework before you applied; now you want to just double-check your original impressions.

Wait List: What Next?

Besides being accepted or rejected, you might be wait-listed. Colleges use their wait lists for different purposes:

- An institution may put some legacies on the wait list as a courtesy, rather than rejecting these applicants outright. Some use the wait list as a way of showing "respect," to a certain high school that usually sends many students to that college.

- A school may rely heavily on the wait list to balance out certain factors and characteristics of the incoming class. A college can then selectively pick students off the list. For example, if the geographic distribution of the incoming freshman class is heavily weighted toward students from the south, the admissions committee may favor a wait-listed student from the northwest rather than one from Alabama.

- A college may use the wait list to maintain class size. For example, one college found that they had underestimated their yield, or how many students would actually enroll, the previous year. The school then had to scramble to find adequate housing for all the incoming freshmen. The following year, the college deliberately underaccepted from the applicant pool so it could better gauge the class size before bringing the freshman class size up to the projected number by pulling from the wait list.

Although being wait-listed is better than being outright rejected if you really do want to attend a particular college, there are some students who would prefer an outright rejection than be in limbo on a wait list. Even if you decide to try and get off the wait list, you still have to go through the steps of accepting another college and will quite likely have to send in a nonrefundable deposit. Should you then get off the wait list of your first-choice college and choose to attend, you forfeit your deposit.

For whatever reason you have been put on the wait list, you will have to decide how important it is to you to move from the list to the accepted student category. If you are happy with the other choices you have in colleges and don't want to bother with the wait list, send back the card and indicate that you no longer want to be considered for admission.

May 1 is the deadline most colleges set for accepting their offer of admission. If you have not been accepted by your wait-list school, you must accept one of the colleges that has offered you a place. But since some schools move quickly to their wait list, hold off until April 30 before sending in your acceptance letter and deposit to the alternative school you have chosen.

While pursuing your wait-list colleges, be sure to visit the other schools that have accepted you and that you are considering attending. In other words, get on with your life as if you are planning to enroll in one of the schools where you have a firm acceptance while at the same time, actively pursue your wait list school(s) as outlined in the following section.

If you still do want to attend a particular college that has wait-listed you, it's time for you to do a significant sell job—with the full understanding that you may not be successful. Here's what you need to do:

- Ask the college's admissions staff if they anticipate going to the wait list and how many students moved off the list in the previous year. At many competitive colleges, there are years when no one is taken off the wait list. The institution may have adequately anticipated its yield and accepted enough students to meet their class projections.

- Some schools rank their wait list. If the school you want to attend does so, you can ask where you stand on the list. But other institutions review the list for each admit. You want to know how the college handles wait list students.

- If the school anticipates going to its wait list, ask to whom you should send a letter indicating your strong desire to attend the college. Send back any official forms, but you will also want to send a personal letter making your case. You want to make clear to them why College X is your first-choice school, how the school is a good match for you, and what you hope to contribute if accepted. Include any new honors or information that makes you a stronger candidate since your application. Make it clear, if you can, that if accepted you will attend. This may be an ethical problem if you are asking more than one college to take you off the wait list, so don't make a promise you can't keep. Instead, state your case for admission as strongly as possible.

- Work closely with your guidance counselor. Advise him of the letters you are sending and give him copies. Ask him to follow up with the college admissions representative. If there is a school that is clearly your first choice, ask him to reiterate your intention to attend if accepted.

- If you have someone whose letter of recommendation will strengthen your case, then by all means, ask him to write to the admissions office. But just like with your original application, these extra letters should be personal and add something new to your file.

- Follow up with weekly phone calls to the admissions office(s). Some schools cut off the wait list by the end of June; others continue to take students off the list until school begins.

- *Remember:* If you are taken off the wait list, it's unlikely that you will get any financial aid. Those dollars have already been allocated. You should talk to the financial aid office, once you have been admitted, to see if you are eligible for any funding, possibly for second semester, and certainly for the following year.

Bottom line: First, you need to decide if you are going to pursue admission at a college that has put you on their wait list. If you do, be persistent and creative. But if you have not heard from your wait-list school(s) by the acceptance date deadline, make a choice and accept a college from those that have offered you admission. That way, you will have a school to attend in the fall. Should you eventually get into your wait-list college, you can always forfeit your deposit at the previously accepted school.

Deferred Admission

Some colleges will admit students but require that they delay their entry to the school until the second semester. This is a tough call. First, it means that you will not enter with all the other incoming freshmen. Not only will you miss the orientation program, but more important, you will miss the bonding experience of entering with your fellow classmates and enjoying the first months of college together. It's unlikely that you will get financial aid, and your roommate and dormitory assignment will be limited. You will need to find something to do for the fall semester until you go to school in the spring. Some students opt to attend another college program for the first semester, some choose the relatively inexpensive local community college, others spend the first semester at another school that has offered them admission, and some choose to work or travel.

Since all schools lose some students in the first semester, deferred admission gives colleges an opportunity to maintain a full class. Furthermore, there are always a few students who fail to show (some having gotten off the wait list at another school and elect to go there). But if this is your first-choice dream school, deferred admission is an option you should consider.

Bottom line: Continue to call the college throughout the summer to see if you can change your entry date.

Worst-Case Scenario

Remember that you always have the option of transferring should your choice of college not work out. If you find that you have made the wrong decision and that you and the college are not a good fit, you can always change schools. Some students have even done so after the first semester, although most finish out their freshman year and transfer as sophomores. In fact, some competitive schools are easier to get into as transfer students than as freshmen. That's because now you have college grades and recommendations from college professors to demonstrate your ability to handle academic challenges. Even if you are unhappy at college, keep your focus on your work. A high GPA will strengthen your transfer application.

College Paperwork

Once you've accepted and sent in your deposit if your school requires one (a few schools don/t), you will be inundated with more paperwork from the college. Get a file folder and keep all the material together. Carefully note on the front of the folder the various deadlines and check them off as you return each document. Keep a copy of each document you return, along with the check number if you have had to send in a payment with a form.

Some of the forms you will have to complete include the following:

- Food plan
- Roommate questionnaire/dormitory preferences
- Summer orientation programs
- Academic registration
- Medical forms/insurance coverage
- Money matters

Here's what you need to know.

Food Plan

At some schools you must take the eating plan that involves three square meals a day—whether or not you've eaten breakfast in the last five years or not. At other colleges you can sign up for a certain number of meals per week. Still others allow you to pay a certain amount of dollars into an account with a certain amount deducted for each meal eaten. At some schools you are assigned to a certain dining hall, while at others you can eat anywhere on campus.

Before you sign up for a food plan, you need to consider the following:

- Be honest with yourself and your eating habits. Don't sign up for a breakfast, lunch, and dinner plan if you never eat breakfast or if you have a lunchtime class or usually study in the library during your lunch hour.
- Does the college give any advice on the typical freshman eating plan? If you are an athlete, do you eat with your team? Is the meal plan different?

- Do you have an option of changing the plan for the second semester if it's not working out for you?
- What happens to any leftover portion of a eating plan account?
- Where can you use your dining card? Can it be used in restaurants surrounding your campus?
- How are the meals served? Is it an all-you-can-eat buffet or are you assigned one entree, two veggies, and a dessert? Suppose you want seconds? Thirds?

Roommate Questionnaire/Dormitory Preferences

Your freshman year roommate(s) may end up being your best friend for life, someone you hope never darkens your doorstep again, or a perfectly fine roommate and nothing more. Colleges use roommate questionnaires in different ways, and you should ask the admissions office how much attention will be paid to your answers. Some have elaborate computer programs that try to match as carefully as possible your preferences with a compatible roommate. In other schools, it basically comes down to smoking or nonsmoking.

Generally, roommate questionnaires, in addition to the smoking issue, try to assess your neatness quotient, music preferences, and sleeping schedule (early riser? night owl?). You should try and be as honest as possible in your responses. One student admitted he fudged on how neat he kept his surroundings for fear he would be match with someone as big a slob as he was. But that really misses the point. There's no advantage to living with a neat freak if your casual attitude toward cleaning up is going to be a source of constant irritation.

You may also be asked to list your preferences for certain on-campus dorms. At some schools there is a considerable variety in the types of dorms and their location on campus. You may get to choose whether you want an all-freshmen dorm or one that houses both under- and upper-classmen. You may get to choose whether you live in a single-sex dorm or one that is co-ed. Perhaps you prefer a substance-free dorm. When you visit the campus during Pre-Frosh Days, be sure to check out the dormitories.

You may also have the option of choosing to have a single room, rather than living with a roommate. Although it will probably be easier to study if you have a single, remember that living with other people is part of the college experience. Before you opt for a single, find out how they are integrated in the dorm. In one college, several floors were composed of single rooms, and the hallway became the de facto social center. In another school, the dorm was divided into suites that consisted of two single rooms, a double, a shared common room, and a shared bathroom.

Even if you have always had your own room at home, you may find it easier to have a roommate than you think. It's fun to have someone else to share the first-year experience with. Don't worry if your roommate isn't your best friend. Actually, sometimes the best roommate experience is with someone who is generally easy to live with but who is not necessarily someone you want to hang out with. That way you both have your own lives but are respectful of your living space.

Be sure to ask the admissions office how easy it is to make a change once you are on campus. Some schools pride themselves on offering students the opportunity to change roommates with no hassle. Others refuse to allow any roommate changes.

Summer Orientation Programs

Almost all schools offer orientation programs for incoming freshmen. Some bring in groups of students at different points during the summer. Others set aside the week before school starts for orientation. Even if it means juggling your summer schedule or family vacation, don't miss freshman orientation. It's an important opportunity to get to know the school, meet your advisor, register for classes, and begin meeting your classmates.

Some colleges offer students the opportunity to go on a hiking/camping trip. In small groups, usually led by upperclassmen, the freshmen get to enjoy the great outdoors while they learn to bond as a group. If you like nature, this can be a fun way to start school.

But know your limits. If you think camping is the Holiday Inn instead of the Hyatt, this may not be the best start for you. No one wants a whiner on a camping trip, and there are no guarantees of good weather.

On the other hand, if you're up for a challenge and can be a good sport if conditions are less than ideal, this trip can create lasting memories and forge wonderful friendships.

Academic Registration

You will be offered the opportunity to register for classes before school starts. Some colleges have a rigid core curriculum in which your choices are limited as a freshman. In other institutions, you'll have some basic distribution requirements, but then a wide array of classes that will fulfill your prerequisites. And in yet other colleges, there are no distribution requirements, and you may be overwhelmed by the choices you can make.

When you visit during Pre-Frosh Days, ask current students about the best courses and the most outstanding professors. Sit in some classes to get a feel for how they are taught. Check the campus bookstore to see if there is student evaluation course guide with reviews of classes and profs. But remember, as always, to keep these reviews in perspective. What bothers one student may not bother you.

Meet with your academic advisor, if at all possible, before registering for classes. Call the dean of students if you haven't been notified who your advisor will be. Ask if there is a "shopping period" for classes. This is usually the first two weeks of school, when you can add and drop courses without any penalty.

Bottom line: The first semester is a period of transition. Although you shouldn't take a full load of easy classes, don't weigh yourself down with a demanding schedule. You have enough to do getting adjusted to college. You want to enjoy yourself as well as learn.

Medical Forms/Insurance Coverage

Schedule an appointment with your doctor for a full checkup, and have him complete your medical form. Many schools require that the physical examination is done within four months of entering college, so if your last checkup was more than that, you'll need to make a follow-up visit.

Make sure all your immunizations are up to date. In addition to the standard vaccinations against measles, mumps, rubella, tetanus, whooping cough, hepatitis, and polio that all students are required to have, the Centers for Disease Control and the American College Health Association recommend that students, especially those living in close quarters like dormitories, be vaccinated against bacterial meningitis. Freshmen living in group housing have six times more risk for the disease than other students.

You and your parents need to decide whether you want to carry the college's health insurance. While you can continue to be covered by your family's plan as long as you are a full-time student, you may also want to be insured under the college's health insurance plan. If you decide not to carry the college's health insurance, you will be asked to sign a waiver.

Ask your parents to check with their health insurance administrator concerning coverage before waiving the college plan. They will want to get the following information from their insurance administrator:

1. How does their health insurance plan …
   - Define emergency services?
   - Cover follow-up medical care? Would you have to return to your own network for follow-up coverage?
   - Cover diagnostic tests and procedures if ordered by a college physician?
   - Handle the deductible or out-of-network co-insurance?
2. What are the requirements for seeing an out-of-network doctor?
3. Does their plan restrict you to certain doctors or hospitals?
4. Does their plan cover mental health care away from home? Are there any restrictions or limitations?

Bottom line: If you waive the college health insurance plan, keep a copy of the waiver and double-check that the health insurance fee has been deducted from your tuition bill.

Money Matters

Before you ever set foot on campus to begin your freshman year, you'll get a bill for the first semester. Review it carefully and make sure you understand what each charge represents. Specifically, check for the following:

- Are you paying for the meal plan you elected?
- If you've waived the college health insurance plan, has that charge been deducted?
- Have you been credited with the financial aid you were offered?
- If you have won any outside scholarships, have they been credited to your account?

Your parents will also have the chance to enroll in a tuition payment plan. For a small fee, they can extend the tuition payments over the year. That is another piece of paperwork to be completed!

You will also receive information from banks near your college, inviting you to open an account. You will have to decide if you want to use your hometown bank or open an account in a bank near campus. There are advantages and disadvantages to each plan.

Hometown bank:

- More convenient for your parents to deposit money.
- No need to change accounts during vacations and summer.
- Unless there is a branch near campus, you may be charged an additional fee for not using your bank's ATM. These fees can add up over a month.
- You'll have to write your local address and phone number on every check before most places will accept it.
- Check with the bursar's office about the school's policy on cashing out-of-town checks with college identification. The office can probably advise you about the check-cashing policy of area businesses.

Bank located near college:

- More convenient for you.
- May have an ATM on campus.
- Area businesses may be more willing to accept local bank checks.
- If your parents are giving you monthly checks for expenses, drawn on a different bank, it may take up to a seven business days for the checks to clear. Will this cause you a cash flow crunch?

Credit Cards

You'll also start receiving offers from credit card companies. It's easy to get a walletful of credit cards while in college. A dorm address and telephone number are just about all you need despite the fact that you don't have an income. But you have to be very careful, because it's easy to get in over your head and ruin your future credit rating, which can affect your insurance and employment. Having a credit card, however, can be helpful in case of emergencies, and if it is in your own name and handled responsibly, can start to build your own solid credit history.

At many colleges, credit card companies set up tables at the most crowded intersection on campus where every student passes several times a day. They offer free T-shirts, water bottles, and other giveaways to encourage students to stop and sign up. But ask yourself if a free T-shirt is worth ruining your future credit.

Credit Card Facts

- One third of students get a general purpose credit card in their own name before entering college.
- VISA is the dominant brand, followed by MasterCard, Discover, and American Express.
- It's easy to run up a bill: 42 percent of students who have a credit card carry a balance forward each month. The average monthly balance is $577.
- One third of student credit card holders use their cards at least once a week, if not more often.

You and your parents have to decide whether to get you a credit card in your own name or to add you as an authorized user of one of their cards.

If the card is in your own name, the bills will be mailed to your school address or to your home address. You will begin your own credit history, so it's critical to pay your bills in a timely fashion. Your credit limit generally is low in the beginning ($300), but once you have proven your credit-worthiness, the limit will be increased regularly and without your asking.

If you become an authorized user on one of your parents' credit cards, you will have a higher credit limit. You can even have your name on the card, although using this card will not build your own credit history.

Add to Your College Box

You may want to put one final piece of paper in your college box: the acceptance letter to the college you will be attending in the fall (that is if you don't put it on the refrigerator or on your bulletin board!). Congratulations!

What You Need to Know

- While waiting to hear from colleges, keep up your grades. Your counselor must send in mid-year evaluation forms, and those grades can make a difference.

- Once you've received your letters of acceptance, try and visit each of the colleges to see the school from the perspective of an admitted student. Check out the other students, the dorms, and other college facilities, as well as attend some classes.

- If you are wait-listed and still want to be considered for admission, you need to make it clear to the college of your continued interest and ask that your counselor be in contact to make your case.

- Once you have accepted a college, keep copies of all forms and documents you return.

Appendix A
Bibliography

College Admissions—Books

Hernandez, Michele A. *A Is for Admission: The Insider's Guide to Getting into the Ivy League and Other Top Colleges.* Warner Books.

Mayher, Bill. *The College Admissions Mystique.* Noonday Press.

Mitchell, Joyce Slayton. *Winning the Heart of the College Admissions Dean: An Expert's Advice for Getting into College.* Ten Speed Press.

Pope, Loren. *Colleges That Change Lives: 40 Schools You Should Know About Even If You're Not a Straight-A Student.* Penguin USA.

———. *Looking Beyond the Ivy League: Finding the College That's Right for You.* Penguin USA.

College Guides

Barron's Educational Series. *Barron's Best Buys in College Education.*

Fiske, Edward B. The *Fiske Guide to Colleges.* Sourcebooks.

Peterson's Guides. *Peterson's 4-Year Colleges.*

Princeton Review. *Complete Book of Colleges.*

Rugg, Federick K. *Rugg's Recommendations on the Colleges.* Rugg's Recommendations.

SAT I, SAT II, and ACT Prep

See series of books for each test by:

Barron's Educational Series

Kaplan

The Princeton Review

Financial Aid

Cassidy, Daniel J. *The Scholarship Book.* Prentice Hall Press.

College Board. *The College Board Scholarship Handbook.*

Kaplan, Benjamin R. *How to Go to College Almost for Free.* Waggle Dancer Books.

Kaplan. *Scholarships*

Peterson's Guides. *Peterson's Scholarship, Grants, and Prizes.*

Essays

Curry, Boykin. *Essays That Worked: 50 Essays from Successful Applications to the Nation's Top Colleges.* Fawcett Books.

Websites

Standardized Test Prep and General Information

College Board
www.collegeboard.com

Educational Testing Service
www.ets.org

Kaplan
www.kaplan.com

National Collegiate Athletic Association (NCAA)
www.ncaa.org

Princeton Review
www.review.com

Sylvan Learning Center
www.educate.com

Financial Aid

Department of Education
Federal Student Aid Information Center
1-800-4-FED-AID
www.ed.gov/prog_info/SFA/

Fast Web
www.fastweb.com

FinAid
www.finaid.com

Mapping Your Future
www.mapping-your-future.org

Scholarship Resource Network Express
www.srnexpress.com

WiredScholar
www.wiredscholar.com

Military

Air Force ROTC
www.afoat.af.mil/rotc.htm

Army ROTC
www.armyrotc.com

Navy ROTC
www.cnet.navy.mil/nrotc/nrotc.htm

Appendix B
Glossary

accepted   You're in! Congratulations! Slang for an offer of admissions from a college.

ACT   Pronounced *A-C-T*, this is the name of the standardized test used by some colleges as part of admissions prerequisite. The test measures English, math, reading, and science reasoning.

Advanced Placement   Also known as AP. College-level courses taken in high school for which students can gain college credit or advanced standing. Students take a College Board exam at the end of each course, and the result may be a factor weighed in the college admissions process.

campus-based programs   These are U.S. Department of Education federal student aid programs, like the Federal Perkins Loan, Federal Supplemental Educational Opportunity Grant (FSEOG), and Federal Work-Study, that are administered by colleges.

College Board   Nonprofit organization that owns various standardized tests, including PSAT, SAT I, SAT II, and AP exams.

College Scholarship Service/Financial Aid PROFILE   The financial aid application service of the College Board. It supplements the FAFSA (Free Application for Federal Student Aid) and is used by 450 colleges and universities as well as 350 scholarship programs. Although you can receive state and federal aid just by completing the FAFSA, some colleges require the CSS/PROFILE to receive institutional money. You can apply online or through a form requested from the College Board.

consolidation loan   This combines one or more of your federal loans (Stafford, PLUS, SLS, FISL, Perkins, Health Professional Student Loans, NSL, HEAL, or Guaranteed Student Loans) into one new direct loan from a single lender. How does this help? It reduces the size of your monthly payment by extending the term of your loan beyond the 10-year repayment plan. Some can be extended up to 30 years, but the amount of interest you will eventually pay is increased.

deferred   The college is unwilling to accept you as an early decision or early action candidate but will consider your application along with the others in the regular decision pool.

direct loans   A federal program that permits schools to act as the lending agency and manage the loan funds directly—the money is from the federal government, but not all schools participate.

Division I (D-I)   Athletic classification by the NCAA. These are the big schools, the ones that you see on television each weekend, playing in front of huge crowds in mammoth stadiums. They are the big time in college athletics. Division I schools are also responsible for meeting minimum financial aid awards for their athletes. The Ivy League is the lone exception to this rule, because there are no athletic scholarships available at Brown, Columbia, Cornell, Dartmouth, Harvard, Penn, Princeton, and Yale.

Division II (D-II)   Athletic classification by the NCAA. These schools are much different than D-I colleges. They are similar in that scholarships are allowed, but it is rare for students to get full scholarships from the athletic department, because D-II athletic programs are financed in the school's budget like any other academic department on campus. More frequently, D-II athletes will get a partial scholarship and pay for the rest of their costs through grants, loans, and work-study earnings. D-II schools are defined by certain scheduling restrictions and are a great opportunity for top-notch local and regional athletes who may not be able to make their way on to the teams at the D-I level.

Division III (D-III)   Athletic classification by the NCAA. Student-athletes at D-III schools play for the love of the game and little else. Crowds can be small at these schools, and the university treats the athletic program just like every other department. There are no athletic scholarships available and coaches have limited recruiting budgets.

early action   Similar to early decision, but with one critical difference. The student applies to a college, usually by November 1 or 15. Colleges agree to notify the applicant of their decision to admit, defer, or reject within six weeks. But the decision to admit is not binding on the student. If admitted, the student still has the option of applying to other schools. Among the Ivy League schools, only Harvard offers an early action program. The remaining Ivies—Brown, Columbia, Cornell, Dartmouth, Princeton, University of Pennsylvania, and Yale—now offer only a single early decision option. Georgetown University, Boston College, University of Chicago, Massachusetts Institute of Technology, and the University of Notre Dame, among others, offer an early action option.

early decision   The student applies to a college with the understanding that if she is admitted, she will attend. Usually, the application deadline is either November 1 or 15. Colleges agree to notify applicants of their decision to admit, defer, or reject by mid-December at the latest. This gives students enough time, should they be deferred or rejected, to send in applications to other colleges. Some institutions have a second (or even third) cycle of early decision applications with early January or February deadlines and responses within six weeks.

Educational Testing Service   National organization that focuses on educational testing and research. They are responsible for designing and administering the College Board tests.

expected family contribution (EFC)   This is how much a student and his parents are expected to pay toward his education. The amount depends on family earnings, assets, how many students in the family are currently in college, and family size. It doesn't necessarily correlate with the reality of how much your family can actually afford to contribute. A FAFSA must be filed to get an EFC.

FAFSA (Free Application for Federal Student Aid)   This is the application that students and parents must complete for almost all forms of student aid. It's available at high schools and colleges, at www.fafsa.ed.gov, or by calling 1-800-4-FEDAID.

Federal Direct Student Loan Program (FDSLP)   These federal loans are provided to students and their parents through the college or university.

Federal Family Education Loan Program (FFELP)   These federal loans are provided to students through private lenders such as banks, credit unions, and savings and loans.

Federal Stafford Loan   Federally guaranteed loans with low interest. There are two types: **subsidized,** which are awarded on a need basis, and **unsubsidized,** which are awarded on a nonneed-basis. For both types, payment can be deferred until the student is out of school, but for unsubsidized loans, interest accrues while the student is still in school. However, the student can defer paying the interest until he graduates. All students are eligible for an unsubsidized Stafford loan, regardless of income; however, you must first file a FAFSA.

Federal Work-Study   A federally sponsored program that pays some of the student's salary for part-time school-year employment. Jobs can be in school departments or businesses. Eligibility is need-based.

grant   Aid that does not have to paid back.

Ivy League   Eight colleges—Brown, Columbia, Cornell, Dartmouth, Harvard, Princeton, University of Pennsylvania, and Yale—are considered the Ivy League. They are extremely selective in admissions.

legacy   The applicant has a close relative who is a graduate of the college. Each school determines their own criteria for being a legacy, which may include parent or grandparent as a graduate or a sibling who is a current student at the college. Each institution also decides how much to weigh legacy as a factor in admissions.

merit-based aid   Nonneed-based aid, merit-based aid is given on the basis of artistic, academic, athletic, or other criteria. This normally does not have to be paid back but may have certain restrictions or requirements (such as maintaining a certain GPA) for the student to continue receiving aid.

National Collegiate Athletic Association (NCAA)   An organization of intercollegiate athletics; a clearinghouse for college athletes.

Pell Grant   A federal grant program. The money does not have to be paid back.

Perkins Loan   A federal loan program that has a low interest rate and is granted on a need basis.

PLUS Loans (Parent Loans for Undergraduate Students)   A federal loan that permits parents to borrow up to the difference between what the education costs and what the financial aid package covers. Parents must begin repayment of loans within 60 days after disbursement. The life of the loan can be spread out over many years to reduce the monthly payments, but this increases the total amount repaid because of the accrual of interest.

PSAT/NMSQT   The Preliminary SAT/National Merit Scholarship Qualifying Test is more commonly known as the PSAT. It may be taken as practice in ninth and tenth grades, but results only count when taken in junior year. According to the College Board, the PSAT measures verbal reasoning skills, critical reading skills, math problem-solving skills, and writing skills.

regular decision   When a student applies to colleges by a set deadline (which varies from school to school). For many private colleges, the application deadline is January 1 for regular decision, but it may be later at some schools. Colleges respond sometime in late March or early April. The student can then choose among all the colleges that have offered him admission.

rejected   You've been denied admission to a college you applied to. Your file is closed.

rolling admissions   Admissions decisions are made as the applications are read, and this continues until the class is filled. Decisions are generally made within six weeks of when the application is filed, however, some public universities choose to place out-of-state applicants in a decision pool for the spring. If applying to a large state university, where rolling admissions is most common, send in those applications early, since the schools often fill their housing and main campus fast.

SAT I   Pronounced *S-A-T,* this standardized test measures verbal skills and mathematical reasoning.

SAT II   Also called achievement tests, these multiple-choice tests are designed to measure a student's knowledge or skills in a particular subject, for example, history or biology.

scholarship Financial aid that does not have to be repaid.

selectivity A college's selectivity index is determined by measuring how many students have applied as compared to how many have been accepted.

subsidized loan A financial aid loan on which students don't have to pay interest until the grace period expires.

Title IV programs This is a group of Federal Student Aid programs including Pell Grants, Federal Supplemental Educational Opportunity Grants, Federal Work-Study, Federal Perkins Loans, Federal Stafford Loans, Federal PLUS Loans, Direct Loan, Direct PLUS Loan, and SSIG.

unsubsidized loan A financial aid loan in which interest accrues while a student is still in school.

wait list A list of students who have applied to a college but who, although qualified, have not been offered admission nor have they been rejected outright. These students may be admitted after the college receives notice from those accepted in the regular decision cycle and can determine if additional students are needed to complete the class.

yield An index that measures how many students actually accept a college's offer of admission as compared to how many were offered admission.

Index